GW00729170

Microsoft Works®
Quick Reference

Douglas J. Wolf

Library of Congress Catalog Number: 90-64386

ISBN 0-88022-694-3

94 93 92 91   4 3 2

Interpretation of the printing code: the rightmost double-digit number is the year of the book's printing; the rightmost single-digit number is the number of the book's printing. For example, a printing code of 91-4 shows that the fourth printing of the book occurred in 1991.

This book is based on Microsoft Works Version 2.0.

Que Quick Reference Series

The *Que Quick Reference Series* is a portable resource of essential microcomputer knowledge. Whether you are a new or experienced user, you can rely on the high-quality information contained in these convenient guides.

Drawing on the experience of many of Que's best-selling authors, the *Que Quick Reference Series* helps you easily access important program information.

The *Que Quick Reference Series* includes these titles:

1-2-3 Quick Reference
1-2-3 Release 2.2 Quick Reference
1-2-3 Release 3 Quick Reference
1-2-3 Release 3.1 Quick Reference
Allways Quick Reference
Assembly Language Quick Reference
AutoCAD Quick Reference, 2nd Edition
C Quick Reference
CorelDRAW Quick Reference
dBASE IV Quick Reference
DOS and BIOS Functions Quick Reference
Excel Quick Reference
Hard Disk Quick Reference
Harvard Graphics Quick Reference
MS-DOS Quick Reference
Microsoft Word Quick Reference
Microsoft Works Quick Reference
Norton Utilities Quick Reference
PC Tools Quick Reference, 2nd Edition
Q&A Quick Reference
Quattro Pro Quick Reference
QuickBASIC Quick Reference
Turbo Pascal Quick Reference
UNIX Programmer's Quick Reference
UNIX Shell Commands Quick Reference
Windows 3 Quick Reference
WordPerfect Quick Reference
WordPerfect 5.1 Quick Reference

iv

Publisher
Lloyd J. Short

Series Product Director
Karen A. Bluestein

Production Editor
Cindy Morrow

Technical Editor
Donald A. Ayre

Production Team
Betty Kish
Jill Bomaster
Scott Boucher

Table of Contents

Introduction

Microsoft Works Quick Reference is not a rehash of traditional documentation. Instead, this quick reference is a compilation of the most frequently used functions and commands from Microsoft Works.

Microsoft Works Quick Reference includes the quick reference that you need to work with Microsoft Works' word processor, spreadsheet, database, and communications modules. This book contains the necessary information to design and use databases, spreadsheets, and graphs; create and print documents; and connect with other computers.

This book is divided into several sections. The first section provides the basic information that you need to work with Microsoft Works, as well as an extensive listing of the shortcut keys available in the program's different modules. The second section provides an alphabetized command reference of the major commands and functions used in Works. The third section supplies detailed information on creating and using macros.

Because it is a quick reference, this book is not intended to replace the extensive documentation and tutorials that are included with Microsoft Works. If you are new to Microsoft Works, you can complement this quick reference with Que's *Using Microsoft Works*.

Now you can put essential information at your fingertips with *Microsoft Works Quick Reference*—and the entire Que Quick Reference Series!

Hints for Using This Book

As you read this book, keep the following conventions in mind:

Words that you type and keys that you press appear in **boldface blue** type. For example,

Type **Board Meeting at 3:00** and press **Enter**.

For this example, you would type the words **Board Meeting at 3:00** from the keyboard and then press the **Enter** key.

To follow a procedure that instructs you to select an item from a menu, such as

Select **A**larm Clock

you can select the item three different ways. First, you can use the cursor-movement keys to highlight the selection from the specified menu and press **Enter**. Second, you can simply type the boldface letter. In this case, you would press **A**. Third, if you use a mouse, you can move the mouse pointer to the selection on-screen and double-click.

Information that you see on-screen appears in a `special` typeface.

MICROSOFT WORKS

Software programs began by being like the learned professor who knows a great deal about one topic. Initially, computer programs could perform many tasks in only one area.

Microsoft Works is, in contrast, an integrated program that enables you to do a lot of work with several different components. You can consider Works the handyman of software programs.

Microsoft Works provides five essential tools that are common to most computer users: word processing, spreadsheets, databases, graphics, and communications. When you start Microsoft Works, you can open an existing file or create a new one. When you select the Create New File option, Microsoft Works lists the types of files that you can create.

Word Processor

The word processor enables you to create documents such as letters, memos, and reports. It includes a spell-checker and thesaurus, search and replace feature, and a bookmark capability. You can add footers, add headers, and modify fonts to emphasize certain words or entire paragraphs. Because of the integrated nature of Microsoft Works, you can copy text from one document to another very easily.

Spreadsheet

Spreadsheets enable you to arrange data in rows and columns and analyze data using arithmetic functions. Generally, you use spreadsheets to analyze financial data in documents such as income statements, balance sheets, and cash-flow statements. The ease and speed of computerized calculations enable you to add complex financial projections, invoices and quotations, and statistical information to the data. You can create "what-if" scenarios easily—when you change one piece of information, the entire spreadsheet adjusts automatically to reflect the change.

The Works spreadsheet files are compatible with other powerhouse spreadsheet programs, which enables you to share information with other spreadsheet users. The graphs, or charts as Microsoft calls them, are interactive with the data in the spreadsheet; if you change the data in the spreadsheet that is displayed graphically, the chart also changes.

Database

A database is a collection of related information. Databases enable you to organize the information that you need in a relevant, convenient form. An example of a database would be a list of important names and telephone numbers that you keep in a book on your desk. Microsoft Works enables you to place these important lists on the computer so that you can access the information more quickly.

The Works database is a flat-file database management program. To use the database, you must first design a form to capture the information. Once you enter the data, you can retrieve, sort, edit, analyze, and delete it as you want. A part of the database module is the report generator, which gives you a detailed look at the database information.

Communications

One of the salient features of using computers is the ability to communicate with other computers. Microsoft Works enables you to connect your computer to another computer, an on-line information service, a user service, and many other national and local networks.

Works dials the phone number and establishes the electronic dialog (referred to as *handshaking*). Unfortunately, no industry standards are in place currently regarding handshaking with another computer. Therefore, Works enables you to integrate the individual communication "protocols" for each computer.

HOW TO USE THIS BOOK

Because Microsoft Works consists of four distinct computer tools in one software package, this Quick Reference includes a subhead under each boxed command that refers you to a specific Microsoft Works application or applications. The subhead tells you which tool to select to achieve the desired result.

For example, you see *Word Processor* under the boxed command header *Undo*. This subhead tells you that you can use the Undo command in Works' Word Processor only. Commands containing the subhead *All* indicate that the command is applicable for all tools in Works.

The final part of this quick reference includes a more detailed discussion of creating and using macros in Microsoft Works.

MENU SHORTCUTS

The Microsoft Works menu structure helps you to navigate through the program. After you learn the structure of the program, however, you may want to use the menu bypassing shortcuts. These shortcuts bypass the menus and take you from one function to another.

Shortcuts for all Works modules

Key(s)	Function
F1	Displays Help screen.
Shift-F1	Displays Help tutorial.
F3	Moves selection.
F5	Accesses the Go To command.
F6	Displays next pane.
Shift-F6	Displays previous pane.
F7	Repeats search.
Shift-F7	Repeats copy or format.
Ctrl-;	Inserts current date.
Ctrl-:	Inserts current time.
F8-→	Extends selection right.
F8-←	Extends selection left.
F8-↑	Extends selection up.
F8-↓	Extends selection down.
Ctrl-End	Goes to end of file.
Ctrl-Home	Goes to beginning of file.
Ctrl-F6	Goes to next window.
Ctrl-Shift-F6	Goes to previous window.

Shortcut keys in spreadsheets and charts

Key(s)	Function
Ctrl-'	Copies contents of preceding cell.
F2	Edits formula.
F9	Recalculates cells.

Key(s)	Function
Shift-F10	Views Chart.
F10	Views spreadsheet.
Ctrl-F8	Selects spreadsheet row.
Shift-F8	Selects spreadsheet column.
Ctrl-Shift-F8	Selects entire spreadsheet.
Tab	Goes to next unlocked cell.
Shift-Tab	Goes to previous unlocked cell.
Ctrl-PgDn	Moves right one window.
Ctrl-PgUp	Moves left one window.
Shift-F5	Goes to next named range.

Shortcut keys for the database

Key(s)	Function
F2	Edits.
F9	Views form/list.
Shift-F10	Views report.
F10	Quits reporting.
F10	Applies query.
Ctrl-F8	Selects record/row.
Shift-F8	Selects field/column.
Ctrl-Shift-F8	Selects entire database.
Tab	Goes to next unlocked field; in Form view, goes to next field.
Shift-Tab	Goes to previous unlocked field; in Form view, goes to previous field.
Ctrl-PgDn	Moves right one window.

Key(s)	Function
Ctrl-PgUp	Moves left one window.
Ctrl-PgDn	Goes to next record in Form view.
Ctrl-PgUp	Goes to previous record in Form view.

Shortcut keys for the word processor

Key(s)	Function
F8, twice	Selects word.
F8, three times	Selects sentence.
F8, four times	Selects paragraph.
F8, five times	Selects entire document.
Shift-F8	Collapses selection.
Ctrl-→	Moves right one word.
Ctrl-←	Moves left one word.
Ctrl-↓	Moves down one paragraph.
Ctrl-↑	Moves up one paragraph.
Ctrl-PgDn	Goes to bottom of window.
Ctrl-PgUp	Goes to top of window.
Shift-F5	Goes to next bookmark.

Shortcut keys for selecting type styles in the word processor

Key(s)	Function
Ctrl-B	Applies bold.
Ctrl-I	Applies italic.
Ctrl-S	Applies strikethrough.
Ctrl-U	Applies underline.

Key(s)	Function
Ctrl-=	Applies subscript.
Ctrl-+	Applies superscript.
Ctrl-space bar	Returns to normal next.

Shortcut keys for formatting paragraphs in the word processor

Key(s)	Function
Ctrl-X	Formats paragraph in normal style.
Ctrl-C	Centers text.
Ctrl-J	Justifies text.
Ctrl-L	Left aligns text.
Ctrl-R	Right aligns text.
Ctrl-H	Creates hanging indent.
Ctrl-G	Undoes hanging indent.
Ctrl-N	Creates nested indent.
Ctrl-G	Undoes nested indent.
Ctrl-1	Single spaces text.
Ctrl-5	1-1/2 spaces text.
Ctrl-2	Double spaces text.
Ctrl-O	Inserts one line before paragraph.
Ctrl-E	Inserts no lines before paragraph.

Shortcut keys for general editing in the word processor

Key(s)	Function
Alt-Backspace	Undoes last command.
Backspace	Deletes character to the left of cursor.

Key(s)	Function
Del	Deletes character at cursor.
Del	Deletes selection.
Tab	Inserts tab mark.
Enter	Inserts new paragraph.
Ctrl-Enter	Forces page break.
F9	Paginates document.
Shift-Enter	Inserts end of line mark.
Ctrl--	Inserts optional hyphen.
Ctrl-_	Inserts non-breaking hyphen.
Ctrl-Shift-space bar	Inserts non-breaking space.
Ctrl-P	Prints page number.
Ctrl-F	Prints file name.
Ctrl-D	Prints date.
Ctrl-T	Prints time.

COMMAND REFERENCE

The following command reference includes all the commands and features that are available within Microsoft Works. The commands are listed the same way: the command or feature name appears first, followed by the modules for which the command applies, the purpose, the procedures, and any applicable notes.

In some cases, a related topic may also help you with a task. In these instances, the Notes section includes a "See Also" paragraph that directs you to related headings.

Alarm Clock

All

Purpose

Notifies you of appointments.

To start a new alarm

1. Press **Alt** to access the menu bar.

2. From the menu bar, select **O**ptions.

3. From the Options menu, select **A**larm Clock.

    The Alarm Clock dialog box appears.

4. Type the message that details why you set the alarm.

    For example you might type **Board Meeting at 3:00**.

5. In the appropriate boxes, enter the date and time that you want the alarm to sound.

6. Move to the Frequency box and select how often you want the alarm to sound.

7. Press **Alt-S** to set the alarm.

    You can set another alarm now or press **Alt-D** to leave the Alarm Clock dialog box.

To change an existing alarm

1. Press **Alt** to access the menu bar.

2. From the menu bar, select **O**ptions.

3. From the Options menu, select **A**larm Clock.

    The Alarm Clock dialog box appears.

4. Press **Alt-U** to access the Current Alarms box. Move the highlight to select the existing alarm that you want to change.

5. Press **Alt-A** or **Alt-I** to go to the Date and Time fields. Enter the changes that you want to make in these fields.

6. When you finish making changes, press **Alt-C** to access the Change option.

7. You now can set, change, or delete another alarm. Press **Alt-D** when you finish working with alarms.

To delete an existing alarm

1. Press **Alt** to access the menu bar.

2. From the menu bar, select **O**ptions.

3. From the Options menu, select **A**larm Clock.

   The Alarm Clock dialog box appears.

4. Press **Alt-U** to access the Current Alarms box. Move the highlight to select the alarm that you want to delete.

5. Press **Alt-T**.

   The selected alarm is eliminated.

Notes

At the time of alarm, a beep sounds and the message you have entered when setting the alarm displays. You may then **R**eset the alarm to a later time or select **S**nooze to ignore the alarm.

You can set a reminder to signal a one-time-only appointment or to signal you daily, weekdays only, weekly, monthly, or yearly.

Works also displays the alarms that you have already set.

You can set the following options in the Alarm Clock dialog box:

Option	Function
Message	Enables you to enter any message up to 60 characters long. For example, you might enter **Lunch with VP of Sales**. Press **Alt-G** to access this field.

Option	Function
Date	Specifies the date of the alarm. Works accepts the date in these formats: **12/28/91**; **December 28, 1991**; or **Dec 28, 1991**. Enter the date when you want the alarm to sound. If you do not include a date, the alarm sounds at the next occurrence of the specified time. For regular daily appointments, leave the date box blank. Press **Alt-A** to access this field.
Time	Specifies the time of the alarm. Works accepts the time in these formats: **10:30 AM**; **10:30 PM** (or **22:30**); or **10:30**. If you do not enter a time in the box, the alarm goes off at midnight.
Frequency	Enables you to select the interval that you want for the alarm. Select **Alt-O** if you want the alarm to go off one time only, select **Alt-W** for weekdays only, **Alt-M** for a monthly alarm, **Alt-L** for a daily alarm, **Alt-K** for a weekly alarm, and **Alt-Y** for an annual alarm.
Current Alarms	Lists the alarms now set, including the date, time, and message.
Suspend Alarms	Suspends preset alarms. Press **Alt-P** to toggle this option on or off. When off, the alarms that you have set go off at the times you set.
Set	Enables you to add a new alarm to the list. Press **Alt-S** to access this option.

Option	Function
Change	Enables you to change the settings for a particular alarm.
Delete	Deletes an alarm setting.
Done	Enables you to specify that you are finished setting options in the Alarm Clock dialog box.

All

All

Purpose

Selects all the text in a word processing file, all cells in a spreadsheet, or all records in the List View or Report form in the database. In communications, all text in the buffer is selected and communications pause.

To select all text, cells, or records

1. Press Alt to access the menu bar.

2. From the menu bar, choose Select.

3. From the Select menu, choose All.

   All on-screen elements are highlighted.

Apply Query

Database

Purpose

Applies a query that you created previously with the Query command.

To apply a query

1. Press Alt to access the menu bar.

2. From the menu bar, choose Select.

3. From the Select menu, choose Apply Query.

Notes

Use this command to requery the database after you edit it. The most recent query is used.

See also *Query*.

Arrange All

All

Purpose

Arranges the screen so that all open windows are visible.

To see all windows that are open simultaneously

1. Press **Alt** to access the menu bar.

2. From the menu bar, select **W**indow.

3. From the Window menu, select **A**rrange All.

   Works arranges the desktop so that all open windows are visible on-screen.

Notes

The open windows are arranged side-by-side.

When you arrange all windows on-screen, the active window appears in the upper left corner so that you can view other files. You can use the Size and Move options to arrange the windows in a variety of ways. You also can use the Maximize command to view a single window after you have arranged all windows on-screen.

See also *Maximize*, *Move*, and *Size*.

Bookmarks

Word Processor

Purpose

Inserts a hidden marker into your text, which you can name and then access quickly using the Go To command.

To create a bookmark

1. From within a word processing document, move the cursor to where you want to insert the bookmark.

2. Press **Alt** to access the menu bar.

3. From the menu bar, select **E**dit.

4. From the Edit menu, select Bookmark **N**ame.

5. In the Name dialog box, type the name of the new bookmark.

6. Select **C**reate or press **Enter**.

   The bookmark number appears in the text of the document.

To find a bookmark

1. Press **Alt** to access the menu bar.

2. From the menu bar, choose **S**elect.

3. From the Select menu, choose **G**o To.

   The Go To dialog box appears. At the top of the dialog box is the Go To prompt. Below this prompt are the names of the bookmarks that you have created.

4. Type the bookmark name that you want to find or use ↓ to highlight the name of the bookmark.

5. Press **Enter**.

   The cursor moves to the location of the hidden bookmark in the text.

To delete a bookmark

1. Press **Alt** to activate the menu bar.

2. From the menu bar, select **E**dit.

3. From the Edit menu, select Bookmark **N**ame.

   The Bookmark Name dialog box appears.

4. In the Names box, type the name of the bookmark that you want to delete.

5. Press **Alt-T** or move the cursor to the Delete option.

   The selected bookmark is deleted from the list of bookmarks that you created.

6. Press **Alt-D** or move the cursor to the Done option. Press **Enter**.

   The hidden bookmark code is removed from the text.

Notes

Select bookmark names that reflect the subject matter so that you can recognize the marker easily at a later time. For example, suppose that you are writing a 50-page document with several sections on the High-Middle Ages. If you want to mark the first reference to the High-Middle Ages, you might select a bookmark such as **Viking**.

Remember to delete bookmarks that have become useless within the document.

See also *Go To*.

Border

Word Processor

Purpose

Draws lines or a box around a paragraph.

To add borders to a paragraph

1. From the Select menu, use the All or Text command to select the paragraph to which you want to add lines or boxes.

2. Press **Alt** to access the menu bar.

3. From the menu bar, select Format.

4. From the Format menu, select Borders.

   The Border dialog box appears.

5. In the dialog box, select the options that you want for the borders.

   An X appears in the parentheses leading your choice.

6. Select OK or press Enter.

Notes

You can select the type of border that you want. The border can be a complete outline or box around the selected paragraph(s), or it can be a line drawn across the Top, at the Bottom, on the Left, or on the Right of the paragraph(s). You also can specify Normal, Bold, or Double-lined borders.

See also *All* and *Text*.

Break

Communications

Purpose

Breaks communication with the other computer.

To break communication with another computer

1. Press Alt to access the menu bar.

2. From the menu bar, select Connect.

3. From the Connect menu, select Break.

Note

Use this command when you are unable to log off normally. For example, you may be connected to CompuServe and the BYE command should end the session. If this command does not work, you can use the Break command in Works to end the session.

Calculate Now

Spreadsheet

Purpose

Enables you to specify when formulas are calculated in a spreadsheet. Use this command when automatic calculation is turned off.

To specify that formulas should be calculated

1. Press **Alt** to access the menu bar.

2. From the menu bar, select **O**ptions.

3. From the Options menu, select **C**alculate **N**ow.

   Formulas are calculated in the spreadsheet.

Note

See also *Manual Calculation*.

Calculator

All

Purpose

Calculates numerical values on-screen, like a handheld calculator. You then can insert the calculated values into your documents.

To calculate a numerical value

1. Press **Alt** to access the menu bar.

2. From the menu bar, select **O**ptions.

3. From the Options menu, select **C**alculator.

4. Press the number and corresponding operator symbol for the calculation that you want to make.

5. With the cursor on the equal (=) sign, press **Enter**.

   The result of the calculation appears at the top of the on-screen calculator.

   For example, if you type **90+90** and press **Enter**, the calculator displays 180.

To insert a calculated numerical value

1. Select a cell or space in which you want the calculated number to appear.

2. Press **Alt** to access the menu bar.

3. From the menu bar, select **O**ptions.

4. From the Options menu, select **C**alculator.

5. Using the keyboard, press the number and corresponding operator symbol for the calculation that you want to make.

   For example, if you type **90+90** and press **Enter**, the calculator displays 180.

6. Press **Alt-I** to insert the calculated value into the preselected cell or space.

To insert a value from a spreadsheet into the calculator display

1. From within the spreadsheet, use the cell selector to highlight the value that you want to display.

2. Press **Alt** to access the menu bar.

3. From the menu bar, select **E**dit.

4. From the Edit menu, select Copy.

5. Press **Alt** again to access the menu bar.

6. From the menu bar, select **O**ptions.

7. From the Options menu, select Calculator.

   The selected value is displayed on the calculator.

Notes

In addition to the standard numerical and arithmetic operator keys, the on-screen calculator also contains the following special keys:

Key	Function
CHS	Changes the sign of the displayed number.
CL	Clears all calculator entries.
CE	Clears only the last entry.
Insert	Inserts the displayed number into the active file at the location of the cell pointer.

Capture Text

Communications

Purpose

Saves to a file text that is transmitted by another computer.

To capture text

1. While connected to a host computer, press **Alt** to access the menu bar.

2. From the menu bar, select **T**ransfer.

3. From the Transfer menu, select **C**apture Text.

   The Save File dialog box appears.

4. Enter the name and extension that is appropriate to the Works module in which you want to open the file.

   For example, if you are capturing a spreadsheet, add the extension .WKS; a word processing file, add .WPS; and a database file, add .WDB.

5. Select OK or press **Enter**.

6. If the file already exists, either use the Append command to add the new data to the file or select a new file name.

Notes

After saving the file, you can open it with the appropriate Works module.

See also *Open Existing File*.

Cells

Spreadsheet, Database

Purpose

Selects a group of cells in the spreadsheet or selects records in the List or Report views in the database. You then can reformat the entire selection.

To select a group of cells or records

1. Use the **Shift**-arrow key combination to highlight the place in the spreadsheet or database where you want to begin selecting.

2. Press **Alt** to access the menu bar.

3. From the menu bar, choose Select.

4. From the Select menu, choose Cells.

   EXT appears on the lower right portion of the screen. This notation indicates that the cell selector is in Extend mode, meaning that the cell selector will stretch across or down cells as you direct it.

5. Use the arrow keys to select the spreadsheet cells or range in the database that you want.

   You also can use the Go To command to extend the range.

6. Press **Esc** to stop selecting.

Notes

You can use the **F8** shortcut key to begin the selection process.

See also *Go To*.

Check Spelling

Word Processor

Purpose

Alerts you of misspelled words, incorrectly capitalized words, incorrectly hyphenated words, and repeated words.

To check spelling

1. Press **Alt** to access the menu bar.

2. From the menu bar, select Options.

3. From the Options menu, select Check Spelling.

4. Works begins going through the word processor document and looking for incorrect words. If it finds a word that it does not recognize, it displays that word in a Check Spelling dialog box.

5. Select an option for remedying the unrecognized word. You can select from the following options:

   • Replace the word with the correctly spelled word.

   • Change all occurrences of the misspelled word (press **Alt-H**).

   • Ignore this instance of the word (press **Alt-I**).

   • Ignore the word each time it is found in the file (press **Alt-G**).

   • Ask Works to suggest some other spellings for the word.

   • Select a word from the list of suggestions and then press **Alt-C** to change the word.

   • Add the word to the Works dictionary (press **Alt-A**).

   Works continues with the spell check until you have determined what to do with each misspelled word or until you select Done from the Check Spelling dialog box.

Notes

In addition to misspelled words, Works alerts you of incorrect capitalization (such as *MIcrosoft*), incorrect hyphenation (such as *hyp-henated*), and repeated words (such as *the the*).

Works moves forward when checking spelling, starting with the cursor location and moving to the end of the file.

All words that Works flags are not necessarily incorrect; they simply are not recognized by the system. Words such as personal names or company names are flagged, also. However, when Works flags names, abbreviations, or terms that you use in your normal activities, you may add them to your personal dictionary. Once added, Works no longer flags those words as suspect.

Close

All

Purpose

Closes the current file and removes it from the screen.

To close a file

1. Press **Alt** to access the menu bar.

2. From the menu bar, select **F**ile.

3. From the File menu, select **C**lose.

   If you have made changes to the file that you have not saved, Works asks whether you want to save the changes. Select Yes or No.

   The file closes. Any remaining open files appear on-screen.

Caution

Never shut off Works without first closing all open files. If you have a power failure or accidentally shut off your computer with open files, you could damage the files and render them unusable.

Notes

You do not have to close the file on which you are working before opening another file or creating a new file. Works permits you to open many files simultaneously, which remain in discrete windows. All open files remain on the desktop, and you can arrange these files on-screen using the Arrange All, Maximize, Move, and Size commands.

If you have open files on the desktop that have been modified and you use the File, Exit commands, before Works closes the modified files, it prompts you with a dialog box asking whether or not you want to save the file with the changes.

See also *Arrange All*, *Maximize*, *Move*, *Save*, and *Size*.

Column

Spreadsheet, Database

Purpose

Selects entire columns in the spreadsheet or in the Report view of the database.

To select an entire column

1. Move the highlight to the column that you want to select.

2. Press **Alt** to select the menu bar.

3. From the menu bar, choose Select.

4. From the Select menu, choose Column.

Note

After selecting the column, you can reformat or edit the column.

Column Width

Spreadsheet

Purpose

Sets the on-screen display width of spreadsheet columns.

To widen a column

1. From within the spreadsheet, use the arrow keys to move the highlight to the column that you want to widen.

2. Press **Alt** to access the menu bar.

3. From the menu bar, select Format.

4. From the Format menu, select Column Width.

5. Enter the character width that you want. The character width is the number of characters across the column.

6. Press **Enter**.

Notes

By default, columns are 10 characters wide.

If you want to widen several contiguous columns, press and hold the **Shift** key and then press the arrow keys to select the columns. Follow steps 2 through 5 to set the width.

An entry that is wider than the width of the cells spills over into the cells to the right if the adjoining cells do not contain entries. If the adjoining cells do contain entries, a series of pound signs (#) appears in the cell that is too narrow.

Communications

Communications

Purpose

Specifies the baud rate, data bits, stop bits, parity, handshaking, and the port to which the modem is connected.

To use the Communications option

1. Press **Alt** to access the menu bar.

2. From the menu bar, select **O**ptions.

3. From the Options menu, select Communications.

   The Communications dialog box appears.

4. Make the appropriate settings in the dialog box.

   A dot appears in the parentheses leading each option that you select.

5. When you finish making selections, choose OK or press **Enter**.

Notes

The Communications dialog box contains the following options:

Baud Rate is the transfer rate of your modem. For example, if your modem is designated as 2400 Baud, enter 2400. The rates can vary from 300 to 2400, and the default rate is 1200.

Data Bits is determined by the computer system that you intend to call. The most common settings are either 7 or 8.

Stop Bits is determined by the computer system that you intend to call. The most common setting is 1.

Parity allows an internal auditing process to check whether enough bits are being sent in the correct amount. An asterisk (*) appears in place of the character whenever an error occurs. To avoid confusion, Works has a Mask setting that enables the program to work with any other computer's setting. The most common setting is None.

Handshake is determined by the computer system that you intend to call and refers to the computers' electronic handshake when they get together. If you are using a modem, the best setting is Xon/Xoff. If a direct cable connection is made, the Hardware setting is appropriate. Select None only if you know that the other computer to which you will be communicating does not have a handshake method.

Port is the physical location of your modem. If your computer is outfitted with two ports for serial communications, you must specify which port is being used for the modem. COM1 is the normal setting.

Setting the Communications settings correctly is the major obstacle to using the computer to communicate with other computers. To perform the setup properly, you must first know your modem rate of data transfer and the protocols for the computer to which you are connecting. If you do not know the protocols, you can experiment with the settings while you are on-line.

Connect

Communications

Purpose

Dials the number that has been entered as part of the
communications file and sends the setup protocols
needed by the other computer.

To communicate with another computer

1. Press **Alt** to access the menu bar.

2. From the menu bar, select **File**.

3. From the File menu, select **File**.

4. Use the File menu and the **Open** command to select
   the communications file that you created previously,
   which contains the number that you want to dial.

5. Press **Alt** again to access the menu bar.

6. From the menu bar, select **Connect**.

7. From the Connect menu, select **Connect**.

Notes

You must first create a communications file before you
can attempt to call another computer.

To create a communications file, use the Options menu
and the Phone command to enter a phone number. After
doing so, save the file under a name that relates to the
phone number. For example, you might save
CompuServe as COMPU.WCM.

See also *Phone*.

Convert

Word Processor

Purpose

Converts a Works word processing file to a different
word processor file format.

To convert a word processing file

1. Press **Alt** to access the menu bar.

2. From the menu bar, select **F**ile.

3. From the File submenu, select Convert.

   Works displays the File dialog box.

4. Type the name of the file that you want to convert, including the extension, or use the arrow keys to highlight the file name. Press **Enter**.

   Works displays a dialog box with a list of file formats to which the file you selected may be converted. Press **Tab** to move the cursor to the format options, and then use the arrow keys to move to the specific format. Before selecting the conversion format, you can direct that the file be saved to a different directory and under a new name. For example, if you want the file to be named CONVERT.WPS and saved on a floppy disk, you could type A:CONVERT.WPS.

5. Name the file and select the conversion.

6. Convert to a different directory by moving the cursor to the Directory dialog box and selecting an alternate directory.

7. Select the format to which you want to convert the file by moving the cursor to the Format box. You can select Microsoft Works, Microsoft Word, Microsoft RTF, or IBM DCA.

Notes

You may convert a Works word processing file to a Microsoft Word file, a Microsoft Interchange Rich Text Format (RTF) file, or an IBM Document Content Architecture (DCA) file. You may also convert a word processing file from those formats to a Works file.

Microsoft does not ship all the conversion programs with Works automatically. If a message displays on-screen that says that the program is not found by Works, contact your dealer or Microsoft.

Copy

All

Purpose

Copies text in the word processor and communications, a cell or range of cells in the spreadsheet, or a field or field label in the database.

To copy information in the Word Processor or in Communications

1. Press **Alt** to access the menu bar.

2. From the menu bar, choose Select.

3. From the Select menu, choose the Text option.

4. Use the arrow keys to highlight the text that you want to copy. Text is highlighted on-screen.

5. Press **Alt** and select Edit.

6. From the Edit submenu, select Copy.

7. Move the cursor to the location where you want to copy the information and press **Enter**.

   The text is copied to the cursor location.

To copy information in the spreadsheet

1. Press **Alt** to access the menu bar.

2. From the menu bar, choose Select.

3. From the Select menu, choose the part of the spreadsheet that you want to copy. You can copy Cells, Rows, Columns, or All.

4. Press **Alt** and select Edit.

5. From the Edit submenu, select Copy.

6. Move the cursor to the location where you want to copy the information and press **Enter**.

   The cells, rows, or columns that you highlighted are copied to the cursor location.

Caution

Always save a file before you start the copying procedures and, unless you want to replace certain data, leave blank space in which to copy data.

Notes

The Copy command creates a copy of the information that you can insert into a new location without deleting it from the original location. Use the Move command to delete the information from the original location and insert it into the new location.

You can press **Shift-F7** to repeat the copy commands. This means that you can copy the same data several times in different files or different parts of a file, while having selected the data only once.

See also *Move*.

Copy Special

Word Processor, Spreadsheet

Purpose

Copies the format of the text characters or paragraphs in the word processor. In the spreadsheet, copies the cell contents but not the cell formulas.

To copy formatting in the word processor

1. Use the Select option to select the character with the text format that you want to copy.

2. With the formatted text highlighted, press **Alt** to access the menu bar.

3. From the menu bar, select **E**dit.

4. From the Edit menu, select Copy Special.

5. Move the highlight bar to the location where you want the format to begin.

6. Select the text to which you want to copy the formatting.

7. Select Edit, then select Copy Special.

   A dialog box appears.

8. Select either Character format or Paragraph format, depending on the type of formatting that you have to copy. Press Enter.

   The new format is inserted into the specified location.

To copy formatting in the spreadsheet

1. Use the Select option to select the cells with the values that you want to copy.

2. Press Alt to access the menu bar.

3. From the menu bar, select Edit.

4. From the Edit menu, select Copy Special.

5. Select the range of cells that you want to copy, beginning with the upperleft cell in the range.

6. Select Edit, then select Copy Special.

   A dialog box appears.

7. Select the option that you want from the dialog box. You can select Values only, Add values, or Subtract values.

8. Select OK or press Enter.

Notes

The Copy Special command is a powerful tool for consolidating identically structured spreadsheets. As an example, if you were calculating the total sales of a company that had three sales regions, and you had created an identical spreadsheet for each region, you could consolidate the sales results for the entire company with the Copy Special command. To do so, you would use the Copy command to create a master spreadsheet and then use the Copy Special command to add the results from each region to the master.

See also *Copy*.

Create New File

All

Purpose

Creates a new file.

To create a new file

1. Press **Alt** to access the menu bar.

2. From the menu bar, select **F**ile.

3. From the File menu, select Create New File.

   A dialog box appears that contains the file options.

4. Select the type of file that you want and press **Enter**. You can create a new Word Processor, Spreadsheet, Database, or Communications file.

   If you decide not to create a new file, select Cancel.

Delete

Word Processor, Database

Purpose

In the word processor, deletes the character at the cursor or the selected text. In the database, deletes a blank line.

To delete text in the word processor

1. Press **Alt** to access the menu bar.

2. From the menu bar, choose **S**elect.

3. From the Select menu, use the arrow keys to highlight either Text or All. The Text choice enables you to extend the highlight using the arrow keys to select the text that you want to delete. Press **Enter**.

4. Press **Alt** to access the menu bar.

5. From the menu bar, select **E**dit.

6. From the Edit menu, select Delete and press **Enter**.

   Works deletes the text.

To delete a blank line in the database

1. Press **Alt** to access the menu bar.

2. From the menu bar, choose **Select**.

3. Use the arrow keys to move the cursor to the blank line that you want to delete.

4. Press **Alt** to access the menu bar.

5. From the menu bar, select **Edit**.

6. From the Edit menu, select **Delete** Line and press **Enter**.

   Works deletes the blank line.

Notes

Use the Delete command to delete whole lines or sections of text. To delete single characters or words, use the **Del** key.

If you delete text accidentally in the word processor, you can use the Undo command to reverse the mistake. You cannot reverse a deletion in the database.

See also *Undo*.

═ **Delete Row/Column**

Spreadsheet

Purpose

Deletes a row or column of information in a spreadsheet. Usually used to modify the appearance of the spreadsheet.

To delete a row or column

1. From within the spreadsheet, use the arrow keys to move the highlight to the row or column you want to delete.

2. Press **Alt** to access the menu bar.

3. From the menu bar, select **Edit**.

4. From the Edit menu, select **Delete** Row/Column.

5. From the Delete Row/Column menu, select to delete either a row or column and press **Enter**.

   Works deletes the row or column.

Caution

Be careful not to delete range references when using this option. If you delete range references, your formulas may be affected by the deletion.

Notes

You can use the Delete Row/Column command to enhance the appearance of your spreadsheets. For example, if you have Year-End totals in a column, and that column is three columns away from the December column, you might want to delete two of the columns to better identify the totals to their respective line items. The same is basically true for deleting rows. A series of labels, such as the months of the year, running across the top of the spreadsheet might be too far away from the initial row of numbers. In either case, when you delete a row or column, Works adjusts the spreadsheet and any formulas that may have extended across the deleted row or column.

If you are deleting a row or column for appearances only, and the deletion does not include any cells with data or formulas, you are on safe ground. However, if you delete cells that contain formula references, you may corrupt the spreadsheet results. Before deleting the Row or Column, save a copy of the spreadsheet so that you have a copy of the old version before you make a drastic change.

Dial Again

Communications

Purpose

Redials the phone number of the active communications file.

To redial the phone

1. Press **Alt** to access the menu bar.

2. From the menu bar, select Connect.

3. From the Connect menu, select Dial Again.

Notes

You must already have opened a communications file to use the Dial Again command.

Dial This Number

Word Processor, Spreadsheet, Database

Purpose

Dials a number through your modem that you select in a spreadsheet, word processing, or database file. This command is used simply to dial the phone so that you can talk; it is not used to connect you to another computer.

To dial a number from a word processor file

1. With the cursor on highlight, select the number that you want to dial.

2. Press Alt to access the menu bar.

3. From the menu bar, select Options.

4. From the Options menu, select Dial This Number.

    Works dials the number.

5. Pick up the receiver.

6. Select OK or press Enter to continue the phone call. If you do not want to continue the phone call, select Cancel.

7. Hang up the phone when the call is complete.

To dial a number from a database or spreadsheet file

1. With the cursor on highlight, select the cell that contains the number that you want to dial.

2. Press Alt to access the menu bar.

3. From the menu bar, select Options.

4. From the Options menu, select Dial This Number.

   Works dials the number.

5. Pick up the receiver.

6. Select OK or press Enter to continue the phone call.
   If you do not want to continue the phone call, select
   Cancel.

7. Hang up the phone when the call is complete.

Notes

Before dialing, specify the Modem Port and Dial Type
in the Works Settings dialog box. The modem must be
installed.

Your computer dealer can give you more information
about installing and using your modem.

Enhancing Text

Word Processor

Purpose

Changes the text format. You can specify the format of
existing text or text that you are about to type.

To begin typing in a new format

1. At the point where you want to begin typing text in a
   new format, press Alt to access the menu bar.

2. From the menu bar, select Format.

3. From the Format menu, select the format that you
   want and begin typing. You can select from the
   following formats:

   • Plain Text

   • Bold

   • Underline

   • Italic

4. When you finish formatting, press Alt to access the
   menu bar and select the Plain Text command.

To change the format of existing text

1. Select the text for which you want to change the format by using the Text or All command on the Select menu.

2. Press **Alt** to access the menu bar.

3. From the menu bar, select the Format menu.

4. From the Format menu, select the format that you want for the selected text and press **Enter**. You can select from the following formats:

   • Plain Text

   • Bold

   • Underline

   • Italic

Notes

You generally will want to use style changes to emphasize a particular item. When sending letters with the names of your products, for example, you might want the names to appear in italics. In business reports, you might want to make headings bold so that readers recognize them easily.

Be careful not to overdo the formatting in your documents. A small amount of well-placed formatting makes your documents stand out; too much formatting makes them hard to read.

See also *Font* and *Style*.

Exit Works

All

Purpose

Closes all files on the desktop and exits to DOS.

To exit Works

1. Press **Alt** to access the menu bar.

2. From the menu bar, select File.

3. From the File menu, select Exit Works.

Note

Works does not permit you to exit without confirming whether you want to save any unsaved changes that you have made to any open files.

File Management

All

Purpose

Handles file housekeeping chores such as copying, deleting, and renaming files; creating and removing directories; copying and formatting disks; and setting the computer's time and date. Many of the File Management activities are DOS commands that Works simplifies by making them accessible directly from Works.

To manage your files

1. Press **Alt** to access the menu bar.
2. From the menu bar, select **File**.
3. From the File menu, select **File** Management.

   The File Management dialog box appears.

4. Select the option that you want from the dialog box. You can select the following options:

   - Copy File
   - Delete File
   - Rename File
   - Create Directory
   - Remove Directory
   - Copy Disk, Format Disk
   - Set Date and Time

To copy a Works file to another disk

If you want to copy a file that you have created in Works to another disk, select the Copy File option to open the Files dialog box. Type the name of the file you want to copy, including the extension, or use the arrow keys to move the highlight to the name of the file that you want to copy and press **Enter**.

If the file that you want to copy is not in the Works directory, type the path and then the file name. For example, if the file is saved in the D:\WORD directory and is named RESUME.DOC, you would type: **D:\WORD\RESUME.DOC** and press **Enter**.

If you do not remember the exact name of the file, simply type the path, **D:\WORD*.***. The asterisks are DOS wild cards that tell Works to list all the files found in the D:\WORD directory. The list of files then is displayed in the File dialog box. Type the name of the file and its extension or use the arrow keys to highlight the name of the file you want to copy. Press **Enter**. Works next prompts you for a new name for the file. If you only want to copy the file from one directory to another, simply add the path followed by the file name.

To copy an entire floppy disk, use the Copy Disk option and Works displays the list of available floppy disk drives. After you select a drive to copy from, you select the drive to copy to. You cannot use this option to copy all the files from a floppy disk to your hard disk.

Notes

The File Management option precludes your having to use DOS to copy files, delete files, rename files, or format disks; to create or remove a directory; or to set the System Time and Date.

The Format Disk option allows you to format a floppy disk as you need it. If you then need to copy files to a floppy disk and have forgotten to format a disk, you do not have to exit Works to use DOS commands to format a disk.

Use the Set Date and Time option to set the correct date and time in the computer system. Many older computers do not have an internal clock and you must type the time and date when you start your computer session. If you forgot to enter the date and time, however, this option lets you do it without exiting Works.

Fill Down

Database, Spreadsheet

Purpose

Inserts a constant value. In a database, inserts the value in several records into the same field. In a spreadsheet, fills a series of vertical contiguous cells with the value of the top cell.

To insert a value into several records into the same field of a database

1. Use a query to find the records that you want to modify.

2. Press **Alt** to access the menu bar.

3. From the menu bar, select **V**iew.

4. From the View menu, select **L**ist. Works arranges the records in a row-by-row fashion.

5. Move the highlight to the column that you want to modify. Enter the value that you want to copy to the affected records in the top field; leave the highlight in that field.

6. Press **Alt** to access the menu bar.

7. From the menu bar, choose **S**elect.

8. From the Select menu, choose **C**ells.

9. Move the highlight down until all the affected records are highlighted.

10. Press **Alt** to access the menu bar.

11. From the menu bar, select **E**dit.

12. Select the **F**ill Down option.

   The value in the top cell is copied down into all the highlighted records.

To fill a series of vertical cells in a spreadsheet with the value of the top cell

1. Move the highlight to the cell containing the value you want to copy down.

2. Press **Alt** to access the menu bar.

3. From the menu bar, choose Select.

4. From the Select menu, choose Cells.

5. Move the highlight down, highlighting all the cells to which you want to copy the value.

6. Press **Alt** to access the menu bar.

7. From the menu bar, select Edit.

8. From the Edit menu, select the Fill Down command.

   Works takes the value in the top cell and copies it down into all the cells that you have highlighted.

Notes

When you view your database in List view, the fields of each record are stacked vertically. If you have zip codes in a database and the zip code changes, for example, you could use a query to find all the affected records and then use the Fill Down command in List View to change all the affected records in one operation.

In a spreadsheet, you can select several vertical cells as the top cells. Then you would move the highlight down to cover the cells below those top cells and use the Fill Down command to fill all the cells in the same operation.

You can copy cell values across from left to right and from top to bottom.

See also *Fill Right* and *Query*.

Fill Right

Spreadsheet

Purpose

Fills a series of horizontally contiguous cells from left to right with the value in the leftmost cell.

To fill spreadsheet cells to the right

1. Move the highlight to the cell containing the value that you want to copy.

2. Press **Shift**-→ to highlight the series of cells in which you want to copy the value.

3. Press **Alt** to access the menu bar.

4. From the menu bar, select **E**dit.

5. From the Edit menu, select Fill **R**ight. Works immediately fills the cells with the value in the leftmost cell.

To copy an entire column of numbers from left to right

1. Position the highlight on the column that you want to copy to the right.

2. Press **Alt** to access the menu bar.

3. From the menu bar, choose **S**elect.

4. From the Select menu, choose the **C**olumn command. The entire column is now highlighted.

5. Press and hold the **Shift** key and then press → to extend the highlight across the columns to which you want to make a copy.

6. Press **Alt** again to access the menu bar.

7. From the menu bar, select **E**dit.

8. From the Edit menu, select Fill **R**ight.

    Works now fills all the columns with the data in the leftmost column.

To copy cell values

1. Press **Alt** to access the menu bar.

2. From the menu bar, choose **Select**.

3. Use the extension selection menu option to designate the cells from which you want to copy.

4. Press **Alt** to access the menu bar.

5. From the menu bar, select **Edit**.

6. From the Edit menu, select Fill **Right**.

   The range of cells that you specified is filled with the designated value or characters.

Notes

You can copy cell values across from left to right and from top to bottom.

See also *Fill Down*.

Fill Series

Spreadsheet, Database

Purpose

Enters a series of values into either vertically or horizontally contiguous cells. For example, you can fill in the names of the months of the year simply by entering **January** and having Works enter the remaining month names.

To enter a series of values into a series of contiguous cells

1. Move the cursor to the cell where you want the series to begin.

2. Type the starting number or date.

3. Press and hold the **Shift** key and press the arrow keys to extend the selection of cells to the cells where you want the values entered.

   The selection highlights on-screen.

4. Press **Alt** to access the menu bar.

5. From the menu bar, select **E**dit.

6. From the Edit menu, select Fill Series.

7. The Units dialog box appears. You can select from the following units:

   • Number
   • Day
   • Weekday
   • Month
   • Year

   If the value that you entered in the first cell is a number, only the Number option is available. If you entered a label, you have the Day, Weekday, Month, and Year options available.

8. If you want the value to increase by more than one, type the value in the Step By box. You can enter either a positive or negative number.

9. Select OK or press **Enter**.

   After making the selection, Works fills the cells with the values that you have designated.

Notes

The step value applies for both numbers and labels. For example, if you want a spreadsheet to list quarterly financial results, you would select Month and then apply a step value of 3. If you began the labels with March, Works would print the labels as March, June, September, and December.

The highlighting remains on after Works enters the values. Therefore, if the values are not what you wanted, you can select the Edit menu and the Fill Series option again and repeat the steps to correct the problem.

Font

Database, Spreadsheet, Word Processor

Purpose

Determines the font that is used when you print a document.

To change the font in a database or spreadsheet

1. Press **Alt** to access the menu bar.

2. From the menu bar, select Format.

3. From the Format menu, select Font.

   A list of available fonts and font sizes appears.

4. Use the arrow keys to select the font that you want from the list.

5. Use the arrow keys to select the font size that you want from the list.

6. Select OK or press **Enter**.

   The font and size that you selected does not appear on-screen, but will print correctly.

To change the font in a spreadsheet chart

1. Select the chart that you want to modify.

2. Press **Alt** to access the menu bar.

3. From the menu bar, select Format.

4. From the Format menu, select Title Font.

   The Title Font dialog box appears. The box contains a list of available fonts and font sizes.

5. Select OK or press **Enter**.

6. To see the fonts on-screen, press **Alt**, select Options, and select Show Printer Fonts.

This option requires a good deal of processing power and, depending on the kind of computer that you have, can significantly slow the on-screen display. If you do not select this option, the fonts that you select do not appear on-screen but do print correctly.

To change the font in a word processed document

1. Press **Alt** to access the menu bar.

2. From the menu bar, select Format.

3. From the Format menu, select Font & Style.

   The Font and Style dialog box appears. The Font box contains the available fonts; the Size box contains the available font sizes.

4. From the Font box, use the arrow keys to select the font that you want.

5. Move to the Size box and use the arrow keys to select the font size that you want.

6. Select OK or press **Enter**.

Notes

The available fonts differ between computers and are determined by the printer to which the computer is connected.

Font sizes are listed in points. One point is equal to approximately 1/72 inch. The actual, physical size of different fonts may vary, even though they have the same size number. Font sizes are determined by measuring the distance between the ascenders (such as the highest point of a *d*) and descenders (such as the lowest point of a *g*) of a font's lowercase letters. Therefore, two different typefaces may have the same font size and appear to be different sizes entirely.

When you select a font, it does not appear on the screen in that format, but will print appropriately. This command changes the font for the entire file.

Footnote

Word Processor

Purpose

Inserts a footnote mark into the text and prints the corresponding footnote text at the end of the text file.

To insert a footnote mark

1. Move the cursor to where you want to insert the footnote reference mark.

2. Press **Alt** to access the menu bar.

3. From the menu bar, select Edit.

4. From the Edit menu, select Footnote.

5. Select the type of footnote reference mark that you want. You can select a numbered footmark or a character mark.

6. Select OK or press **Enter**.

7. Type the footnote in the pane that appears on-screen.

8. Press **F6** to end editing and go back into the text file.

9. Press **Alt** to access the menu bar.

10. From the menu bar, select Options.

11. From the Options menu, select Show Footnotes to close the pane.

To modify a footnote reference mark

1. Move the cursor to the footnote reference mark in either the file or the footnote pane.

2. Press **Alt** to access the menu bar.

3. From the menu bar, select Edit.

4. From the Edit menu, select Footnote.

5. Type the new footnote reference mark by changing from number to character or vice-versa.

6. Press **Enter**.

Notes

After you select this command, the footnote reference is inserted into the text. The footnote pane opens, which permits you to enter the footnote. All footnotes are printed at the end of the text file.

In the footnote, you may use the Insert Special commands to aid in formatting the footnote. Works can number footnotes automatically, or you can specify non-numerical reference marks. When you move, copy or delete a footnote reference mark in your file, Works also moves, copies or deletes the corresponding footnote text and automatically renumbers the footnotes.

To move the cursor back into the text, press **F6**. To move back into the footnote, press **F6** again.

Form

Database

Purpose

Enables you to view a database in form format, which means you can view a single record at a time.

To see the database in form view

1. Press **Alt** to access the menu bar.

2. From the menu bar, select **V**iew.

3. From the View menu, select **F**orm.

   The database records are now arranged in form format. Use the List command to see the records in list format.

Notes

You can view a database in either a form format or a list format. Form view is the default. Use this command to return to form view after looking at the database in list format.

See also *List*.

Format Data

Spreadsheet, Database

Purpose

Formats cells to display numbers as you want them.

To change the format of cells or fields

1. Highlight the area that you want to modify by pressing and holding the **Shift** key and then pressing the arrow keys.

2. Press **Alt** to access the menu bar.

3. From the menu bar, select Format.

4. From the Format menu, select the appropriate format. You can select the following formats:

Format	Effect
General	Formats numbers as precisely as possible. For example, 466 or 4.66 or 4.66E+6.
Fixed	Formats numbers to the number of decimal places that you specify. If you specify three places, a number like 456.7896 becomes 456.790. Any negative numbers display with a leading minus (–) sign.
Currency	Formats numbers to include a leading dollar sign and a comma every three places to the left of the decimal point.
Comma	Formats numbers by separating every three places with a comma. Negative numbers display in parentheses.
Percent	Formats numbers so that they display with a trailing percent sign and the decimal place moves two

	positions to the right. A number such as .0567 becomes 5.67%.
Exponential	Displays numbers in scientific notation. 9999999 displays as 9.99E+.06. An exponent has a range of ±300. Negative numbers display with a leading minus (−) sign.
True/False	Formats cells to display either TRUE or FALSE. All numbers display as TRUE. Cells with zero entries display as FALSE.
Time/Date	Formats cells to display entries as time or date in the format that you specify.

Notes

The general format is integer, decimal. If the number is too large for the cell to display, the number changes to exponential format. For example, 1,000,000 would appear as 10^6.

See also *Time and Date*.

Freeze Titles

Spreadsheet

Purpose

Freezes the row and column headings so that they appear on-screen wherever you move on a large spreadsheet.

To freeze titles

1. Begin from within the spreadsheet document. To freeze rows, move the highlight to the leftmost cell in the row directly below the row headings. To freeze headings, move the highlight to the topmost visible cell in the column to the right of the column headings that you want to freeze.

2. Press **Alt** to access the menu bar.

3. From the menu bar, select **O**ptions.

4. From the Options menu, select Freeze **T**itles.

5. The row or column headings stay stationary as you move within the spreadsheet.

To unfreeze titles

1. Press **Alt** to access the menu bar.

2. From the menu bar, select **O**ptions.

3. From the Options menu, select Unfreeze **T**itles.

Note

You cannot use the highlight to select frozen rows or columns.

Go To

Word Processor, Database, Spreadsheet

Purpose

Moves the cursor to a bookmark or page number in the word processor, a cell or range name in the spreadsheet, or a field or record number in the database.

To go to a location in a word processor document or spreadsheet

1. Press **Alt** to access the menu bar.

2. From the menu bar, choose the **S**elect menu.

3. From the Select menu, choose **G**o To.

4. In the word processor or the spreadsheet, Works displays the names of bookmarks or range names.

5. Select the bookmark or range name to which you want to move.

6. Select OK or press **Enter**.

To go to a location in a database

1. Press **Alt** to access the menu bar.

2. From the menu bar, choose **Select**.

3. From the Select menu, choose **Go** To.

4. In the Go To box, type a record number or a field name of the record or field where you want the cursor located.

5. Select OK or press **Enter**.

Notes

You also can use the **F5** shortcut key to execute the Go To command.

You can insert invisible bookmarks into documents to mark places that you will want to access later. You then can use the Go To command to locate these bookmarks quickly.

See also *Bookmarks*.

Headers and Footers

Word Processor, Database, Spreadsheet

Purpose

Creates headers and/or footers for each page of the file.

You can specify two different types of headers in word processor documents: *paragraph* and *standard*. A paragraph header or footer is text that is formatted like regular text, including tab marks and multiple lines. You can center this text or align it on the right margin. You can specify only paragraph headers and footers in word processor documents.

To create a standard header or footer

1. Press **Alt** to access the menu bar.

2. From the menu bar, select **Print**.

3. From the Print menu, select **Headers** & Footers.

4. In the Header and Footer dialog box, enter the header or footer text.

Works will enter text such as the page number or current date automatically if you specify these options in the header or footer. You can use the following special formatting commands in headers or footers:

Command	Function
&l or &r	Aligns text to the left or right.
&c	Centers text.
&p	Prints page number.
&f	Prints file name.
&d	Prints the current date.
&t	Prints the current time.
&&	Prints an ampersand (&).

5. If you do not want the header or footer to print on the first page, select the No Header on 1st Page or No Footer on 1st Page option.

For example, if you are printing a report with a title on the first page, you would suppress the header on the first page.

6. Select OK or press Enter.

To create a paragraph header or footer

1. Press Alt to access the menu bar.

2. From the menu bar, select Print.

3. From the Print menu, select Headers & Footers.

4. Move the cursor to the Use Header & Footer Paragraphs option. Press Alt-U to turn on the option. An X appears in the box next to the option.

5. Move the cursor to OK and press Enter.

6. Move the cursor up to the H or F at the top of the screen. Enter your header next to the H or your footer next to the F.

7. To add more lines to the header or footer, press **Alt**, select **E**dit, and select Insert **S**pecial.

    The cursor is on the end-of-line mark.

8. With OK highlighted, press **Enter** or **Shift-Enter**. Another H or F, depending on whether you are creating a header or footer, appears on-screen.

9. If you want to insert the current date or the page number automatically, press **Alt**, select **E**dit, and select Insert **S**pecial. Move the cursor to the Print Date option or Print Page option. The header or footer line will display *date* or *page* for the current date or page number, respectively.

10. When you finish creating the header or footer, move the cursor out of the header or footer area and continue typing or editing the text in your document.

To add space when a header is too long

1. Press **Alt** to access the menu bar.

2. From the menu bar, select **P**rint.

3. From the Print menu, select Page Setup & **M**argins.

    The Page Setup & Margins dialog box appears.

4. Move the cursor to the Header Margin option and enter the size of the margin that you want, followed by a ". For example, you might type **2"**.

5. With OK highlighted, press **Enter**.

Removing a header or footer

1. Press **Alt** to access the menu bar.

2. From the menu bar, select **P**rint.

3. From the Print menu, select **H**eaders & Footers.

    The Headers & Footers dialog box appears.

4. Move the cursor to Use Header & Footer Paragraphs and press the **space bar** to turn off the option.

    The X no longer appears before the option.

5. Move the cursor to OK and press **Enter**.

    The header (H) and footer (F) are removed from the top of the file.

Notes

Standard headers or footers are used most often in spreadsheets and databases. These one-line headers and footers are centered automatically, and dates and times are printed in a predetermined format.

The standard margin settings for headers is 1/2 inch. If your header or footer will be more than three lines long, you need to add space in the Page Setup & Margins option on the Print menu.

If you are editing or revising a report regularly, you will probably want to insert the date or time into the header or footer. You then can verify that the document is the latest version.

Hide Record

Database

Purpose

Hides designated records from view on-screen and in reports.

To hide records

1. Press **Alt** to access the menu bar.

2. From the menu bar, select View.

3. From the View menu, select List.

4. Press **Alt** again to access the menu bar.

5. From the menu bar, choose Select.

6. Highlight the records that you want to hide.

7. Press **Alt** again to access the menu bar.

8. From the menu bar, choose Select.

9. From the Select menu, choose Hide Record.

The selected records disappear from the screen and the status line changes to show that one less of the number of existing records is displayed.

Notes

Whereas protecting a database keeps others from changing, rearranging, and editing data, hiding fields or records keeps database information completely confidential.

A hidden record is not listed in List view and does not appear in the Form view. A hidden record cannot be included in a report or printed with other records. The status line displays the number of displayed records compared to the total number of records. If 22/25 appears on the status line, for example, 22 of the total 25 records are displayed; three records are hidden.

Although the records are hidden, you can access them by using the Query or Search commands.

See also *Query*, *Search*, and *Show All Records*.

Indents & Spacing

Word Processor

Purpose

Sets the line spacing and indentations for selected areas of text.

To add space before or after a paragraph

1. Using the Text or All command from the Select menu, highlight the text for which you want to specify spacing.

2. Press **Alt** to activate the menu bar.

3. From the menu bar, select Format.

4. From the Format menu, select Indents & Spacing.

   The Indents & Spacing dialog box appears.

5. Using the cursor-movement keys, move the cursor to `Space before paragraph: [0 li....]`.

6. Enter the number of lines that you want before the selected text.

7. Move the cursor to `Space after paragraph: [0 li....]`.

8. Enter the number of lines that you want after the selected text.

9. Press **Enter**.

Works inserts the designated number of lines before and after the selected text.

To indent selected text

1. Using the Text or All command from the Select menu, highlight the text for which you want to specify spacing.

2. Press **Alt** to activate the menu bar.

3. From the menu bar, select Format.

4. From the Format menu, select Indents & Spacing.

The Indents & Spacing dialog box appears.

5. Using the cursor-movement keys, move the cursor to the option that you want. You can specify the following text indents:

Option	*Function*
Left Indent	Specifies how far the selected text indents from the left margin.
First Line Indent	Specifies how far the first line of the selected paragraph(s) indents from the left margin.
Right Indent	Specifies how far the selected text indents from the right margin.

6. Specify the number of inches that you want to indent the selected text. For example, you might enter .5".

7. When you finish specifying indents, press **Enter**.

Works indents the selected text as you specified.

To create a hanging indent

1. Highlight the paragraph to which you want to apply a hanging indent.

2. Press **Ctrl-H**.

   Works automatically creates a hanging indent with the selected text.

Notes

You can use indentations and spacing variations throughout documents to make certain passages stand out in the text. For example, if you are inserting a long quotation into a document, you might indent the left and right margins 1/2 inch to distinguish the quotation from the rest of the text.

A hanging indent starts the paragraph on the left margin, and the lines that follow the first line have an indentation. You might want to use hanging indents for lists of items. You can then begin each item with an asterisk (*) and tab to make the items stand out.

If you simply want to specify single- or double-spacing for the selected text, you can select Single Spacing or Double Spacing directly from the Format menu.

See also *All* and *Text*.

Insert Chart

Word Processor

Purpose

Inserts a chart into a text file.

To insert a chart into a text file

1. Press **Alt** to access the menu bar.

2. From the menu bar, select **F**ile.

3. From the File menu, select **O**pen Existing File to open the spreadsheet file containing the chart that you want to insert.

4. Use the arrow keys to move the cursor to the location in the text where you want the chart to print.

5. Press **Alt** to access the menu bar.

6. From the menu bar, select **E**dit.

7. From the Edit menu, select **I**nsert Chart.

   The Spreadsheets dialog box appears.

8. In the Spreadsheets dialog box, press the **space bar** to select the spreadsheet file that you want.

9. In the Charts dialog box, select the chart name that you want by highlighting it and pressing the **space bar**.

10. Select OK or press **Enter**.

    Works inserts a placeholder for the chart.

Notes

When you use this command, Works inserts a placeholder into the text that indicates where the chart will print.

To change the size of the chart, move the cursor to the chart placeholder. The Indents & Spacing command on the Format menu enables you to change the chart size.

See also *Indents & Spacing*.

Insert Field

Word Processor

Purpose

Inserts information from a database file to create form letters, mailing labels, and so on. When you insert the field, it acts as a placeholder until you actually print the letter or label.

To insert a database field into text

1. Press **Alt** to access the menu bar.

2. From the menu bar, select **F**ile.

3. From the Edit menu, select Open. Open the database that contains the information that you want to insert into the text.

4. Use the arrow keys to move the cursor to the location in the text where you want the information inserted.

5. Press Alt to access the menu bar.

6. From the menu bar, select Edit.

7. From the File menu, select Insert Field.

8. In the Databases dialog box, select the database that you want to use.

9. In the Fields box, select the appropriate field.

10. Select OK or press Enter.

Works inserts a placeholder into the text.

Notes

When you execute this command, Works inserts a placeholder in the text that designates the field from which the information is to be inserted into the text. Use this command for creating mail-merged letters.

See also *Open Existing File*.

Insert Page Break

Word Processor, Database, Spreadsheet

Purpose

Forces a page break when printing.

To insert a forced page break

1. Move the cursor to the line, column, row, record, or field that you want to begin printing on the next page.

2. Press Alt to access the menu bar.

3. From the menu bar, select Print.

4. From the Print menu, select Insert Page Break.

Works inserts a >> symbol at the page break.

To delete a forced page break in the word processor

1. Move the cursor to the forced page break, placing the cursor directly on the dotted line.

2. Press **Shift-End**.

3. Press **Del**.

   The dotted line symbolizing the page break and the >> symbol disappears.

Notes

Forcing page breaks gives you control over how printed material appears on the page. For example, you might want to force a page break just before a section heading. You then can guarantee that the heading is on the top of the page, not on the bottom of a page with the text following it on the next page.

In the word processor and the Form View of the database, you may only break the pages horizontally. If you insert a page break in a text file, you can delete it by pressing the **Del** key. In the database or spreadsheet, you can delete a page break with the Delete Page Break Print menu command.

See also *Delete*.

Insert Special

Word Processor

Purpose

Inserts special formatting characters into a word processing document.

To insert a special character

1. Use the arrow keys to move the cursor in the text to the location where you want to insert the format character.

2. Press **Alt** to access the menu bar.

3. From the menu bar, select **E**dit.

4. From the Edit menu, select Insert Special.

5. From the dialog box, select the format that you want. You can select from the following options:

Option	Function
End-of-Line-Mark	Starts a new line but not a new paragraph. Use this special character to keep a table or several lines of text together as one paragraph.
Optional Hyphen	Displays a hyphen when a word breaks at the end of a line. If not at the end of a line, the word is not hyphenated.
Non-Breaking Hyphen	Keeps words that must be separated by a hyphen from breaking at the end of a line.
Non-Breaking Space	Keeps words that must stay together from breaking at the end of a line.
Print Page	Inserts a placeholder for the page number. When you print the file, the page number is printed. The placeholder is *page*.
Print File	Inserts a placeholder for the file name. When you print the document, the name of the file is printed. The placeholder is *filename*.
Print Date	Inserts a placeholder for the date the document is printed. The date is printed in the MM/DD/YY format. The placeholder is *date*.
Print Time	Inserts a placeholder for the time the document is printed. The time is printed as HH:MM AM/PM. The placeholder is *time*.

Option	Function
Current Date	Inserts the then-current date into a document and does not update the date as does the Print Date format command. No placeholder is used.
Current Time	Inserts the then-current time into the document and does not update the time as the Print Time format command. No placeholder is used.

6. Select OK or press **Enter**.

Notes

After you insert special formatting characters, Works hides them. To see the characters, access the menu bar, select **Options**, and select Show All Characters.

The special characters that you insert in the text indicate how the document looks when you print it.

See also *Show All Characters*.

Justification

Word Processor

Purpose

Sets the justification for selected areas of text.

To set the justification for an area of text

1. Select the text for which you want to change the justification by using the Text or All command on the Select menu.

2. Press **Alt** to access the menu bar.

3. From the menu bar, select Format.

4. From the Format menu, select the format that you want. You can select from the following options:

Option	Function
Left	Lines up text on the left margin.
Center	Centers text between the left and right margins.
Right	Lines up text on the right margin.

The selected text is justified as you specify.

To justify both sides of the text

1. Select the text for which you want to change the justification by using the Text or All command on the Select menu.

2. Press **Alt-J**.

   The text is justified on both the left and right margins.

Notes

You also can use the following hot keys to specify justification:

Hot key	Effect
Ctrl-L	Left-justifies text.
Ctrl-C	Centers text.
Ctrl-R	Right-justifies text.
Ctrl-J	Justifies both margins.

Line Spacing

Word Processor

Purpose

Sets the line spacing for selected areas of text.

To set the line spacing for an area of text

1. Select the text for which you want to change the justification by using the Text or All command on the Select menu.

2. Press **Alt** to access the menu bar.

3. From the menu bar, select Format.

4. From the Format menu, select the format that you want. You can select either Single Spacing or Double Spacing.

List

Purpose

Enables you to see the database records in list format, which means that you can view multiple records, row by row.

To see database records in list format

1. Press **Alt** to access the menu bar.

2. From the menu bar, select View.

3. From the View menu, select List.

   The database records now are arranged in list format. Use the Form command to see the records in the default form format.

Notes

The default format for viewing database records is form view. Use this command to see a list of the database records in list format.

See also *Form*.

Macros

Purpose

Store lists of commands that you can "replay" with one or two keystrokes. Works enables you to use macros to automate routine, time-consuming tasks.

To create a macro

1. Begin at the place in Works where the macro is to start. For example, if you are creating a database query macro, you would most likely begin in the database file from which you will draw the query.

2. Press **Alt-/** (slash) to open the Macro dialog box.

3. Select Record Macro. Works requires that you specify the combination of keys that will replay the macro. You also need to name the macro.

   The word RECORD appears at the bottom right of the screen. This word indicates that the macro recorder is turned on.

4. Begin entering the keystrokes that execute the routine that you want to save.

5. When you finish recording the keystrokes of the new macro, press **Alt-/** (slash).

To replay a macro

1. Open the file in which you want the macro to execute.

2. Press and hold the **Alt** key and press the key that you used to store the macro.

   The macro executes.

Notes

You can create exotic macros, such as those that pause and wait for keyboard input. You also can create nested macros, where a second macro executes within the first macro.

For more information about macros, see the Macros section at the end of this quick reference.

Manual Calculation

Spreadsheet

Purpose

Enables you to control when formulas are calculated in a spreadsheet, instead of calculating them automatically.

To toggle Manual Calculation on or off

1. Press **Alt** to access the menu bar.

2. From the menu bar, select **O**ptions.

3. From the Options menu, select **M**anual Calculation.

   When toggled on, formulas are calculated only when you specify by selecting the Calculate Now command. When toggled off, formulas are calculated automatically after each entry.

Notes

When Manual Calculation is turned on, the word CALC appears on the bottom screen border. To recalculate a number when manual calculation is on, press **F9**.

See also *Calculate Now*.

Maximize

All

Purpose

Enlarges the current window to fill the entire screen.

To make the current window fill the screen

1. Press **Alt** to access the menu bar.

2. From the menu bar, select **W**indow.

3. From the Window menu, select Ma**x**imize.

   A dot appears in front of the command name in the menu.

   If you use a mouse, click the up/down arrow in the upper right corner of the window to maximize the window.

Notes

When you maximize a window, all open windows are maximized.

The Maximize command is a toggle. If you select it again, the screen is no longer maximized.

Move

Word Processor, Spreadsheet, Database

Purpose

Moves to a new location a block of text in the word processor, a range of cells in the spreadsheet, or a field or field label in the database.

To move information in the word processor

1. Move the cursor to the place in the text where you want to start the selection. Press **Alt** to access the menu bar.

2. From the menu bar, choose **Select**.

3. From the Select menu, choose the **Text** or **All** option. If you use the Text option, use the arrow keys to highlight the text that you want to move. If you use the **All** option, Works automatically highlights the entire document.

   The text highlights on-screen.

4. After selecting the text, press **Alt** to access the menu bar.

5. From the menu bar, select **Edit**.

6. From the Edit submenu, select **Move**.

7. Move the cursor to the location where you want to move the information.

8. Press **Enter**.

   Works moves the text from the previous location to the new location.

To move a cell or range of cells in a spreadsheet

1. Press **Alt** to access the menu bar.

2. From the menu bar, choose Select.

3. From the Select menu, choose the command that you need. To select cells in more than one column or row but not the entire spreadsheet, select Cells. The Cells command allows you to extend the highlight in a cell-by- cell fashion.

4. Press **Alt** to access the menu bar.

5. From the menu bar, select Edit.

6. From the Edit menu, select Move.

   Works returns to the spreadsheet.

7. Move the highlight to the place to which you want the cells, rows, or columns to move.

8. Press **Enter**.

   The cells, rows, or columns that you highlighted move to the cursor location.

To move fields or field labels in the database

1. Position the cursor so that the field or field label that you want to move is highlighted.

2. Press **Alt** to access the menu bar.

3. From the menu bar, select Edit.

4. Depending on what you have selected to move, select either Move Field or Move Label. The Move Field option appears when the Field Label and the Field itself will move together.

5. Position the highlight at the location where you want to move the field.

6. Press **Enter**.

   The field or field label is inserted at the new cursor location.

Caution

Be careful when moving cells that contain cell references. Works attempts to keep the formulas correct, but relative references are often corrupted. It may be prudent to first copy the cells and see whether the references are correct, and then go back and delete the old location.

Notes

When moving fields or field labels in a database, if the field label and the field are immediately adjacent to each other, you can move both in a single operation. If they are not, you must move either the label first and then go back and get the field information or vice-versa.

The Move command deletes information from its prior location and inserts it into the new location. To make a copy of the information that you can insert into a new location while retaining the information in its original location, use the Copy command.

See also *Copy*.

Move

All

Purpose

Enables you to reposition the current window.

To move the current window

1. Press **Alt** to access the menu bar.

2. From the menu bar, select **W**indow.

3. From the Window menu, select **M**ove.

   The lower left corner of the screen is the active window.

4. Use the arrow keys to reposition the window and press **Enter**.

Notes

If you moved the window when it was still in full-screen size, you will be unable to move it far. Use the Size command first to reduce the size of the window, and then use the Move command to reposition it.

Because Works permits you to open eight windows at a time, each containing a unique file, you might want to move windows to different locations on the screen for better viewing. This command is best used after you have reduced the size of the current file window, which enables you to move it greater distances.

See also *Size*.

New Chart

Spreadsheet

Purpose

Enables you to view a chart (graph) that is associated with the spreadsheet.

To view a chart

1. Press **Alt** to access the menu bar.

2. Access the menu bar and select **V**iew.

3. From the View menu, select **N**ew Chart or select a chart that is listed in the menu. You also can select the Charts command and choose Stored Chart.

4. After viewing the chart, press **Esc** to return to the spreadsheet.

Note

When you designate cells for viewing as a chart, you either can press **F10** or use the menu commands to see the chart. In addition, if you have saved charts, you can recall them using this command.

New Reports

Database

Purpose

Creates a report from your database records.

To create a new report

1. Press **Alt** to access the menu bar.

2. From the menu bar, select **V**iew.

3. From the View menu, select **N**ew Report.

4. Press **Esc** to see the report definition.

   When the report definition displays, you can modify the report.

5. Press **Enter** to see additional pages.

6. When you finish looking at the pages, press **Alt** to access the menu bar.

7. From the menu bar, select **V**iew.

8. From the View menu, select the form to which you want to return in the database form view.

Notes

The New Report command permits you to use the pre-existing report that comes with Works or use the pre-designed report as a guide to create your own report.

Works permits up to eight different report formats per database. The report format and its output are saved with the database.

Open Existing File

All

Purpose

Opens a saved file.

To open a saved file

1. Press **Alt** to access the menu bar.

2. From the menu bar, select **F**ile.

3. From the File menu, select Open Existing File.

   A File window appears.

4. At the File window, type the name of the file that you want or use ↑ and ↓ to highlight the file name from the list.

5. Press **Enter**.

   The selected file appears on-screen.

Notes

If the file that you want to open is not in the WORKS directory, select the Drive and Directory at the File window. When the File window opens, press **Tab** twice. The cursor appears in the Directories section of the File window. From here, use ↓ to select drive A, B, C, or D.

If the file that you want to open is not in the WORKS directory, enter the Drive and Directory in the File window. When the file dialog box appears, press **Tab** twice. The cursor is now positioned on the Directories section of the dialog box. Works automatically checks your computer hardware and displays the list of available drives. Use ↓ to position the highlight on the drive where the file is located and press **Enter**. Works now displays the list of files found on the drive that you just selected. Type the name of the file or use the arrow keys to highlight the file name and press **Enter**.

Because of the windowing capability of Works, you might have as many as 14 open files at a time. You can switch from file to file easily.

Page Setup & Margins

All

Purpose

Determines the page layout of the printed output. You can use this option to set the margins for regular letter-sized paper, to specify a different paper size for special printing jobs, or to determine the page number on which you would like the document to begin numbering.

To set margins

1. Press **Alt** to access the menu bar.

2. From the menu bar, select **Print**.

3. From the Print menu, select Page Setup & **M**argins.

   The Page Setup & Margins dialog box appears.

4. Use the cursor-control keys to move the cursor to the margins that you want to change. You can change the following margins:

Option	*Function*
Top Margin	Specifies how close to the top of the page the first line of text prints.
Bottom Margin	Specifies how close to the bottom of the page the last line of text prints.
Left Margin	Specifies how close the text prints to the left side of the paper.
Right Margin	Specifies how close the text prints to the right side of the paper.
Header Margin	Specifies how far from the top of the page the header prints.
Footer Margin	Specifies how far from the bottom of the page the footer prints.

5. When you finish setting margins, select OK or press **Enter**.

   You will see some changes to the screen. When this text prints, it will fit within the specified margins.

To set paper size

1. Press **Alt** to access the menu bar.

2. From the menu bar, select **Print**.

3. From the Print menu, select Page Setup & Margins.

   The Page Setup & Margins dialog box appears.

4. Move the cursor to the Page Length field. Enter the length of the paper.

5. Move the cursor to the Page Width field. Enter the width of the paper.

6. Select OK or press **Enter**.

   The text changes on-screen to fit the page size that you have established.

To set the beginning page number

1. Press **Alt** to access the menu bar.

2. From the menu bar, select **Print**.

3. From the Print menu, select Page Setup & Margins.

   The Page Setup & Margins dialog box appears.

4. Move the cursor to the 1st Page Number field. Enter the page number of the first page of the document.

5. Select OK or press **Enter**.

Notes

After making changes to the page margins, use the Print, Preview command to see how the text will appear when printed.

By default, Works is set up for 8 1/2-by-11-inch paper and specifies the following margins:

Margin	*Default Setting*
Top	1"
Bottom	1"
Left	1.3"
Right	1.2"
Header	.5"
Footer	.5"

If you change the page size and not the margins, the text prints with Works' default margins. If you changed the paper size to 4 1/2-by-6-inch size and didn't change the margins, the document would still print with top and bottom margins of one inch. You might want to decrease margins as you decrease paper size and increase margins as you increase paper size.

You can only offset headers and footers from the left edge of the paper.

See also *Preview*.

Paginate Now

Word Processor

Purpose

Shows you the current location of page breaks in a word processor document.

To paginate a document

1. Press **Alt** to access the menu bar.

2. From the menu bar, select **O**ptions.

3. From the Options menu, select Paginate **N**ow.

   The updated page indicators appear on-screen.

Notes

After invoking the Paginate **N**ow command, use the Print menu and the Preview command to see the effect of the pagination.

Works continually places page breaks in a document, which are indicated by the >> sign. Use the Paginate **N**ow command to ensure updated page breaks.

Pause

Communications

Purpose

Temporarily pauses communication with another computer.

To suspend communication

1. Press **Alt** to access the menu bar.

2. From the menu bar, select Connect.

3. From the Connect menu, select Pause.

Note

Pause works as a toggle. Selecting it once stops communications; selecting it again restarts communications.

Phone

Communications

Purpose

Enables you to enter the phone number and, if necessary, the setup string for a particular service.

To enter a phone number and modem setup string

1. Press **Alt** to access the menu bar.

2. From the menu bar, select Options.

3. From the Options menu, select Phone.

4. Make the appropriate entries in the dialog box. You can select from the following options:

Option	*Function*
Phone Number	Enables you to enter the local number for computer services, such as CompuServe, so that Works automatically dials the number for you when you select the CompuServe communications file. If you are working where it is necessary to access an outside line before dialing the number, add the access number to the beginning of the phone number followed by a comma. The comma pauses the dialing sequence momentarily, then Works dials the rest of the number.
Modem Setup	Holds the series of characters required to initialize your modem, if your modem requires such characters. See your modem manual for details.
Dial Type	Specifies Tone or Pulse dial. The default is Tone. Use Pulse for rotary phone systems.
Automatic Answer	Places Works in auto-answer mode to wait for another computer to call you.

Notes

The communication files are specific for each computer that you want to call. When you create a communication file, the phone number must be for dialing that particular service.

Some computers require that you include a setup string before the number is dialed, which you enter in the dialog box. You also can use this command to place Works in Auto-Answer mode, in which another computer can call you and Works answers the phone and receives any information that is being transmitted.

To save money and use the computer after normal business hours, you can use the Automatic Answer option to wait for another computer to call with information. Suppose that your company has an office on the East Coast and an office on the West Coast. Assuming that you are in the East Coast office, you can set the computer to receive a file from the West Coast office after the normal work day. Leave the computer turned on. After setting the Automatic Answer feature in the Phone dialog box, select the Connect option from the Connect menu. Works waits for the incoming call and takes a message, which will be waiting for you when you come to work the next day. You can therefore extend your workday without being in the office and save money by taking advantage of lower phone rates.

See also *Connect*.

═ Position ═

Word Processor

Purpose

Specifies the position of selected text in a word processor document.

To set the position of text

1. Press **Alt** to access the menu bar.

2. From the menu bar, select Format.

3. From the Format menu, select Font & Style.

   The Font & Style dialog box appears.

4. Move the options in the Position box. You can select from the following positions:

- Normal
- Superscript
- Subscript

5. With the cursor in the parentheses before the option that you want, press the **space bar**.

   A bullet appears in the parentheses, and the text is formatted in the position that you selected.

Preview

All

Purpose

Displays the file on-screen as it will appear when printed on paper.

To preview a file before printing

1. Press **Alt** to access the menu bar.

2. From the menu bar, select **P**rint.

3. From the Print menu, select Print Preview.

4. In the dialog box, you can determine whether to preview the document in draft or final mode. In draft mode, any inserted charts, set microspacing, or specified fonts are not visible.

   Press **Enter** or **Alt-P** to see the document in Preview mode. Works displays the document on the right half of the screen. In the left half of the screen, the portion of the first sentence of the document displays so that you can identify the page. This feature is necessary because the text on the page is not legible in Preview mode.

   Press **Esc** if you want to cancel the Preview.

Note

Use the Preview command to save time and paper by looking at the output before it prints. Preview is especially handy when you are printing lengthy documents.

Print

All

Purpose

Creates paper output of your Works files.

To print a word processor document

1. Press **Alt** to access the menu bar.

2. From the menu bar, select Print.

3. From the Print menu, select Print.

   The Print dialog box appears, which enables you to specify how you want the document printed.

4. At the `Number of copies` prompt, enter the number of copies that you want to print. If you don't enter a value, Works defaults to one copy.

5. Move the cursor to the `Print specific pages` prompt. If you only want to print certain pages of the document, press the **space bar**. An X appears in the parentheses before the prompt.

6. Press **G** to move the cursor to the `Pages` prompt.

   To specify a range of pages to print, enter the first and last pages that you want printed, separated by a dash (−) or period (.). For example, if you want to print pages 20 through 33, you would enter either **20–33** or **20.33**.

   To specify unconnected pages to print, enter each page that you want printed, separated by a comma (,). For example, if you want to print page 20, page 22, and page 25, you would enter **20, 22, 25**.

7. Move the cursor to the `Print to file` prompt. If you want to print the document to a file rather than produce a paper copy, press the **space bar**. An X appears in the parentheses before this option. Enter the name of the file to which you want the document printed.

When you select the Print to File option, a file is created with all the printer commands in it. Therefore, you can print the document from DOS without starting or using Works.

8. Move the cursor to the `Draft quality` prompt. If you want to print in draft—rather than final—quality, press the **space bar**. An X appears in the parentheses before the prompt.

    If you choose to print in draft mode, any charts that you have inserted and any microspacing or fonts that you have set do not print. Draft mode is considerably faster than printing in final mode.

9. Select OK or press **Enter** to print. Select Cancel to cancel the printing.

To print a database report

1. Press **Alt** to access the menu bar.

2. From the menu bar, select **P**rint.

3. From the Print menu, select **P**rint.

    The Print dialog box appears.

4. Move the cursor to the `Number of copies` prompt and enter the number of copies that you want to print.

5. Move the cursor to the `Print all but record rows` prompt. Press the **space bar** if you want to use this option. An X appears in the parentheses before the prompt.

    If you are printing a report, the Print Specific Pages and Print to File options are dimmed, and you cannot select them.

To print a spreadsheet

1. Press **Alt** to access the menu bar.

2. From the menu bar, select **P**rint.

3. From the Print menu, select **P**rint.

    The Print dialog box appears.

4. At the `Number of copies` prompt, enter the number of copies that you want to print. If you do not enter a value, Works defaults to one copy.

5. Move the cursor to the `Print specific pages` prompt. If you only want to print certain pages of the document, press the **space bar**. An X appears in the parentheses before the prompt.

6. Press **G** to move the cursor to the `Pages` prompt.

   To specify a range of pages to print, enter the first and last pages that you want printed, separated by a dash (–) or period (.). For example, if you want to print pages 20 through 33, you would enter either **20–33** or **20.33**.

   To specify unconnected pages to print, enter each page that you want printed, separated by a comma (,). For example, if you want to print page 20, page 22, and page 25, you would enter **20, 22, 25**.

7. Move the cursor to the `Print to file` prompt. If you want to print the document to a file rather than produce a paper copy, press the **space bar**. An X appears in the parentheses before this option. Enter the name of the file to which you want the document printed.

   When you select the Print to File option, a file is created with all the printer commands in it. Therefore, you can print the document from DOS without starting or using Works.

8. Move the cursor to the `Print row and column labels` prompt. If you want the spreadsheet to include row and column labels, press the **space bar**. An X appears in the parentheses before the prompt.

9. Select OK or press **Enter** to print. Select Cancel to cancel the printing.

To print a chart

1. Press **Alt** to access the menu bar.

2. From the menu bar, select **Print**.

3. From the Print menu, select **Print**.

   The Print dialog box appears.

4. Enter the top and left margins.

5. Enter the width and height of the chart.

6. Enter the width and height of the paper on which you're printing.

7. Select either Landscape (chart prints horizontally across the longer access of the page) or Portrait (chart prints with the longest measurement oriented vertically).

8. Select OK or press **Enter** to print. Select Cancel to cancel the printing.

Notes

When you print a spreadsheet, you first must select the print area, because spreadsheets do not follow an 8 1/2-by-11 inch format as a word processing document. For example, if the spreadsheet is a budget for an entire year, it is going to be wider than a normal piece of paper. When the spreadsheet prints, you will probably want to carry over the row and column titles so that you can match the numbers properly. Before you copy row and column labels, use the Print Preview command to look at the spreadsheet as it will appear on paper so that you can determine the location for the labels. Your labels are distinct from the row and column labels. You can print the row numbers 1 through 4,096 and column letters A through IV with Print Row and Column Labels in the Print dialog box.

When you are printing in the database module, the print options change depending on whether you access the Print menu when the database is in List view or Form view. In Form view, you can print a single record at a time. Also, you can set the options to print only the field contents or both the field contents and the field labels. You also can set the option to print more than a single record per page, if space permits. When you designate more than one record per page, you must enter a measurement for spacing between the records.

In List view of the database module, all the records are printed per page, although you can limit the number of pages that print. You also can determine whether or not the field labels print at the top of the columns. Last, in database Report view, you can set Works to print only introductory and summary row types.

If Works does not print your document after you follow the printing instructions, you may have entered the wrong printer or port when you installed the program. Return to the setup program, install a different printer or port, and try again. Refer to your printer manual to make sure that you selected the appropriate model number. If your printer is not listed, select the Works print.file Driver. You also can adjust ports in the Printer Setup dialog box.

See also *Printer Setup*.

Print Form Letters

Word Processor

Purpose

Creates form letters consisting of a text file and a database file. To print form letters, you first must have created a text file with placeholders for database fields.

To create a form letter

1. Press **Alt** to access the menu bar.

2. From the menu bar, select **P**rint.

3. From the Print menu, select Print **F**orm Letters.

   A dialog box appears, which lists the available databases. For a database to be available for printing form letters, you must have opened the database file first.

4. In the Databases dialog box, position the highlight on the database that you want to use as the source and press **Enter**.

   The Print dialog box now appears. You have the option of printing only specific pages of the document, printing to a file, or printing in draft mode.

5. Make your selections in the Print dialog box.

6. Select OK or press **Enter**.

To print a test form letter

1. Open the database file that holds the records that you want to use.

2. Press **Alt** to access the menu bar.

3. From the menu bar, select **F**ile.

4. From the File menu, select **O**pen Existing File.

5. Move the cursor to the database file that you want and press **Enter**.

6. Press **Alt** again to access the menu bar.

7. From the menu bar, select **W**indow.

8. From the Window menu, select the file that contains the form letter that you want to test.

    The form letter appears on-screen.

9. Press **Alt** again to access the menu bar.

10. From the menu bar, select **P**rint.

11. From the Print menu, select **P**rint.

12. Press **Enter** when the Print dialog box appears.

    A copy of the form letter prints on-screen. Instead of displaying the values from the specified database, the letter contains the fields that you created, such as `<<address>>`.

13. Make any changes on-screen.

Notes

When you need to send the same letter to several different people, printing form letters enables you to personalize the letter for each individual on your mailing list. For example, if you are sending out collections letters to those clients with outstanding bills, you can enter the amount that each client owes.

Before printing all the form letters, your best strategy is to print several to determine that the correct information is being inserted into the letter. You also might want to print a test copy of the form letter on-screen so that you can check for accuracy and make sure that you have included all punctuation correctly.

You may want to use the Print Preview option to make sure that the printed letter will look like you want it.

See also *Preview* and *Print*.

Print Labels

Purpose

Prints mailing labels by taking information from a database file and inserting it into a word processing file.

To print mailing labels

1. Press **Alt** to access the menu bar.

2. From the menu bar, select **P**rint.

3. From the Print menu, select Print **L**abels.

4. In the database box, select the database from which you want to get information.

5. In the Vertical field, enter the distance from the top of one label to the top of the next label. For example, you might type **1.5"**.

6. In the Horizontal field, enter the width for a single label. For example, you might enter **3"**.

   If you are printing more than one label across, enter the distance from the left edge of one label to the left edge of the next label.

7. In the Number of Labels Across Page box, enter the appropriate number. The default setting is 1.

8. Press **Alt-T** to run a two-label test.

The Page Setup & Margins dialog box appears. Enter any changes in this box if you have not set the dimensions previously.

9. Press **Enter**.

The Print dialog box appears.

10. Press **Enter** for the test. One label prints.

Notice that you can change the setting for the number of labels to print.

The screen displays `Print all labels or reporting test labels?`.

11. If you are satisfied with the test, highlight Print and press **Enter**.

The Print dialog box appears. Select the options that you want, highlight Print, and press **Enter**.

The labels print.

12. If you are not satisfied with the test, make adjustments, highlight Test, and press **Enter**.

Works prints another test label.

Notes

The test label is the first label in your database. When you print the entire list of labels, the first label is printed again with any adjustments that you have made.

See also *Page Setup & Margins*.

Printer Setup

Word Processor, Database, Spreadsheet

Purpose

Selects the printer that you want to use for the specific print job. After you have set up a printer, it becomes the default printer. You must have installed the printer driver first when you initially installed the entire Works program.

To set up an installed printer

1. Press **Alt** to access the menu bar.

2. From the menu bar, select **P**rint.

3. From the Print menu, select Printer **S**etup.

   The Printer Setup dialog box appears. In it is listed
   the printer(s) from which you can choose to print.
   After selecting the Printer and the Model, you may be
   able to select the level of graphics output. You also
   might switch the Page Feed between Continuous or
   Manual page feeding. Last, you can select the printer
   port. Generally, the port will be LPT1.

4. Select the print options that you want.

5. Select OK or press **Enter**.

Note

The available printer(s) depends upon the printers that
you designated when you installed Works. Using the
setup is distinct from installing a printer.

⇒ Protect Form

Database

Purpose

Protects the design of your database form from certain
changes. When you enable this command, you still can
change the field contents, but not the field sizes or the
field labels. In List view, you also cannot change the
field names.

To protect a database form from changes

1. Press **Alt** to access the menu bar.

2. From the menu bar, select **O**ptions.

3. From the Options menu, select Protect **F**orm. A mark
   is inserted in front of the option, which indicates that
   the form is protected.

   This selection is a toggle; selecting it again turns off
   the protection.

Note

Use this command to insure the integrity of your database form for yourself and for anyone who may enter new data.

Protect/Unprotect Data

Database, Spreadsheet

Purpose

Prevents other Works users from changing database fields or spreadsheet cells.

To protect database information

1. Press **Alt** to access the menu bar.

2. From the menu bar, choose **Select**.

3. In a spreadsheet, select **Cells**, **Row**, **Column**, or **All**.

   In a database, you first may perform a query and select only specified records to be protected. Then use the following steps. If you do not use a query, all records are protected.

4. Press **Alt** to access the menu bar.

5. From the menu bar, select **Options**.

6. From the Options menu, select **P**rotect Data.

   The data is now protected.

7. Select OK or press **Enter**.

To protect spreadsheet information

1. Press **Alt** to access the menu bar.

2. From the menu bar, choose **Select**.

3. Use the Select menu to choose the spreadsheet portions that you want to protect. You can select Cells, **R**ows, **C**olumns, or **A**ll.

4. Press **Alt** to access the menu bar.

5. From the menu bar, select **Options**.

6. From the Options menu, select Protect Data.

   The data is now protected.

7. Select OK or press Enter.

To unlock specific cells in a spreadsheet

1. Press Alt to access the menu bar.

2. From the menu bar, select Options.

3. From the Options menu, select Protect Data. If an asterisk is next to the Protect Data command, select the command again to turn off locking.

4. In the spreadsheet, select the cell or cells that you want to remain unlocked after you again turn on the Protect Data command.

5. With the cell or cells selected, press Alt to access the menu bar.

6. From the menu bar, select Format.

7. From the Format menu, select Style.

   The Style dialog box appears.

8. Press Alt-K to erase the mark in front of the Locked option. Select OK or press Enter.

9. Press the Alt key to access the menu bar.

10. From the menu bar, select Options.

11. From the Options menu, select Protect Data.

Notes

The Protect Data option is a toggle; if you select it once, the data is protected. If you select it again, the data is no longer protected.

Protection of cells or fields is enabled automatically in Works. You must select the fields or cells, however, before they are actually protected.

Query

Database

Purpose

Enables you to locate database records based on the query criteria.

To enter a query

1. Press **Alt** to access the menu bar.

2. From the menu bar, select **V**iew.

3. From the View menu, select **Q**uery.

4. Enter the data in the database form that you want Works to match.

5. Press **Alt** again to access the menu bar.

6. From the menu bar, select **V**iew.

7. From the View menu, select **L**ist or **F**orm to see the matching database records.

   In Form view, use **Ctrl-PgDn** and **Ctrl-PgUp** to see other records.

Notes

Use a database query to look for certain records in your database that meet two or more criteria. If you are going to find records that meet only one criterion, using a search is easier. When you want to find records that have *Canada* in the Country field, for example, use a search. When you want to find records that have *Canada* in the Country field, a purchase amount over $50, and a balance due, use a query.

The result of your query can be a report. You may want to create a report that lists the names of your friends in New York City with more than two children and with whom you have corresponded in the last 12 months. You can create a report that lists the number of employees with degrees in electrical engineering, who have more than 10 years experience with your company, and who are interested in traveling to a new position in Brazil. A query can use any of the data in the fields of your records.

When you select this command, Works displays the
database form and you can enter the data that you want
Works to match.

See also *Form* and *List*.

Range Name

Spreadsheet

Purpose

Creates, changes, or deletes a range name.

To create a named range

1. Use the **Shift** and arrow keys to select a series of
   contiguous cells.

2. Press **Alt** to access the menu bar.

3. From the menu bar, select **Edit**.

4. From the Edit menu, select Range **N**ame.

5. In the Name box, type a range name for the selected
   cells.

6. Select Create or press **Enter**.

To change a named range

1. Open the Range Name dialog box and press ↓ twice.

   The first range name listed appears at the top of the
   dialog box in the Name field.

2. Move the cursor to highlight the range name that you
   want to change.

3. Press **Alt-T** to delete the current range name.

4. Return to the worksheet and repeat the steps to create
   a range name by moving the cursor to the left of the
   text, directly below the text, or in the same cell. Then
   press **Alt**, select **E**dit, and select Range Name.

To change the cell reference for a named range

1. Select the new range.

2. Press **Alt** to access the menu bar.

3. From the menu bar, select Edit.

4. From the Edit menu, select Range Name.

5. Move the highlight until the named range that you want to modify displays in the Name field.

6. Press Alt-C to create the new range.

Notes

Range names make spreadsheet formulas more understandable by identifying the cells that make up the formula. For example, a loan amortization spreadsheet might have cells that contain the interest rate, the term, and the principal amount. In the amortization formula, those components are identified only by the cell ranges in which the values are entered. Linking the cell ranges with a name simplifies the process of building and editing the formulas.

Receive File

Communications

Purpose

Saves an entire file that was sent by another computer using XMODEM protocols.

To receive a file

1. While connected, ask the other computer to send the file using XMODEM.

2. Press Alt to access the menu bar.

3. From the menu bar, select Transfer.

4. From the Transfer menu, select Receive File.

   The Save File box appears.

5. In the Save File box, enter a name for the incoming file.

6. In the Format box, select Binary or Text.

7. Select OK or press Enter.

   The transfer begins.

Notes

The file does not appear on-screen when you use this process; it appears in the File dialog box.

The Works status bar alternates between RECEIVE and WAITING as the file transfers. The process will probably take longer than you expect. At any time during the transfer, you can press Esc to stop the process.

Record Sign-On

Communications

Purpose

Records keystrokes that are used to communicate with a different computer.

To record a sign-on

1. At the point in your communication that you want to record the keystrokes, press Alt to access the menu bar.

2. From the menu bar, select Connect.

3. From the Connect menu, select Record Sign-on.

4. Type the keystrokes as you normally would.

5. When you finish typing keystrokes, turn off the recording by accessing the Connect menu and selecting the Record Sign-on command.

Notes

The Record Sign-on acts as a toggle. Selecting it turns the recording on; selecting it again turns the recording off.

See also *Sign-On*.

Replace

Word Processor

Purpose

Finds and replaces designated text.

To find and replace text

1. Position the cursor where you want to begin the search in the file. If you want to begin at the start of the file, press **Ctrl-Home**.

   You can use the Text command on the Select menu to search only a portion of the file.

2. Press **Alt** to access the menu bar.

3. From the menu bar, choose **Select**.

4. From the Select menu, choose **Replace**.

5. In the Search For box, enter the text that you want to find.

6. In the Replace With box, enter the new text with which you want to replace the original text.

7. Select the Replace options that you want. You can select either Replace or Replace All.

8. Select Replace to activate the Search and Replace function. Works finds the next occurrence and asks you whether you want to replace the text. Select Yes, No, or Cancel.

9. Select OK or press **Enter** when Works finishes finding all occurrences of the text.

Notes

If you are certain that you want to replace all occurrences of the text without being prompted by Works, select the Replace All option.

See also *Search*.

Reports

Purpose

Renames, deletes, or copies a database report. By
default, Works adds a name to a report such as *Report1*
or *Report2*. The Reports command enables you to
replace that designation with a more descriptive name.

To rename a report

1. Press **Alt** to access the menu bar.

2. From the menu bar, select **V**iew.

3. From the View menu, select **R**eports.

   Works displays the list of saved reports.

4. Select the report that you want to rename.

5. In the Name box, type a new name for the report.

6. Select Rename or press **Enter**.

7. Select Done or press **Esc**.

   The report is renamed with the name that you
   specified.

To delete a report

1. Press **Alt** to access the menu bar.

2. From the menu bar, select **V**iew.

3. From the View menu, select **R**eports.

4. From the Reports box, select the report that you want
   to delete.

5. Select Delete by pressing **Alt-T**.

6. Select Done by pressing **Alt-D** or press **Esc**.

   Works deletes the specified report.

To duplicate a report

1. Press **Alt** to access the menu bar.

2. From the menu bar, select **V**iew.

3. From the View menu, select Reports.

    A list of reports appears on-screen.

4. From the reports listed, select the one that you want
    to duplicate.

5. In the Name box, type a name for the duplicate of the
    report.

6. Select Copy by pressing **Alt-C**.

7. Select Done or press **Esc**.

To copy data in a database report

1. With the cursor on the first field that you want to
    copy, press **F8**.

    The status line displays EXT.

    You also can press **Alt**, select **E**dit, and select **C**opy.

2. Use the arrow keys to extend the cursor and highlight
    the area that you want to copy.

3. Press **Shift-F3**.

    The status line displays Select new location
    and press ENTER. Press ESC to cancel.

4. Use the arrow keys to move the cursor to the location
    where you want to insert the copied data and press
    Enter.

    The data remains in the original location and is
    copied to the new location.

Row

Spreadsheet, Database

Purpose

Selects entire rows in the spreadsheet or the Report view
of the database.

To select rows

1. Move the highlight to the row that you want to select.

2. Press **Alt** to access the menu bar.

3. From the menu bar, choose Select.

4. From the Select menu, choose Row.

   The selected row highlights.

Notes

After making a selection, you can reformat or edit the selection.

You also can use the **Ctrl-F8** shortcut key combination to execute this command.

Run Other Programs

All

Purpose

Allows you to exit Works temporarily and run a different application program.

To run a different application

1. Press **Alt** to access the menu bar.

2. From the menu bar, select **F**ile.

3. From the File menu, select Run Other Programs.

   The Programs window appears.

4. Use ↑ or ↓ to select the application that you want to run. Press **Enter**.

   The selected program appears on-screen, while a small portion of Works resides in memory.

5. To return to Works, access the DOS prompt and type **EXIT**.

To set up another application program

1. Press **Alt** to access the menu bar.

2. From the menu bar, select **F**ile.

3. From the File menu, select Run Other Programs.

   The Run Other Programs dialog box appears.

4. Press **Tab** until the Change List command highlights and press **Enter**.

5. Press **Tab** until the Add command highlights.

6. Type the name of the program that you want to appear on the list of available programs.

7. Type the command to start the program.

   For example, if the program is on drive D: in the WORD directory and is called WORD, you would type **D:\WORD\WORD**.

8. Press **Tab** until the Done command highlights and press **Enter**.

   The new program is added to the list. You might find that the program does not run if it uses a great deal of RAM. In that case, you cannot use this option for that particular program.

Note

Before you can use the Run Other Programs option, you must set up the other application programs contained on your computer.

Save

All

Purpose

Saves a new file or an edited file.

To save a file the first time

1. Press **Alt** to access the menu bar.

2. From the menu bar, select **F**ile.

3. From the File menu, select **S**ave.

   The Save As dialog box appears.

4. Enter a file name in the dialog box. File names can be up to eight characters in length, and the extension can be up to three characters in length.

For example, a file name could look like
XXXXXXXX.XXX. The period separates the file
name from the file extension. Works automatically
adds the appropriate extension to files if you do not
specify one. A word processor file automatically
receives the extension .WPS, a spreadsheet receives
.WKS, and a database receives .WBD.

5. If you do not want to save the file in the WORKS
directory, you can include a path.

For example, if you want to save the file on a floppy
disk drive, you can type **A: FILENAME.WPS**.
Works then saves the file FILENAME.WPS on the A
floppy disk drive. You also can save the file in a
subdirectory of the Works directory. You must have
created the directory previously using DOS
commands. If the subdirectory is called LETTERS
and is located under WORKS, you would type
C:\WORKS\LETTERS\FILENAME.WPS.

Works saves the file.

To save a file after the first time

1. Press **Alt** to access the menu bar.

2. From the menu bar, select **F**ile.

3. From the File menu, select **S**ave.

Works saves the file.

Notes

The first time that you save a file, Works prompts you
for a file name. Any time that you save the file after that
time, Works overwrites the existing file with any
changes that you have made since the last save.

The Save option overwrites any existing file of the same
name with the information of the file you are saving.
You can use the Save As option on the File menu to save
a new version of the file without writing over the
original.

See also *Save As*.

Save As

All

Purpose

Saves an edited file under a new file name.

To save a modified file as a new file

1. Press **Alt** to access the menu bar.

2. From the menu bar, select **File**.

3. From the File menu, select Save **As**.

   The Save As dialog box appears.

4. Enter a file name in the dialog box. File names can be up to eight characters in length and the extension can be up to three characters in length.

   For example, a file name could look like XXXXXXXX.XXX. The period separates the file name from the file extension. Works automatically adds the appropriate extension to files if you do not specify one. A word processor file automatically receives the extension .WPS, a spreadsheet receives .WKS, and a database receives .WBD.

5. If you do not want to save the file in the WORKS directory, you can include a path.

   For example, if you want to save the file on a floppy disk drive, you can type **A: FILENAME.WPS**. Works then save the file FILENAME. WPS on the A floppy disk drive. You also can save the file in a subdirectory of the Works directory. You must have created the directory previously using DOS commands. If the subdirectory is called LETTERS and is located under WORKS, you would type **C:\WORKS\LETTERS\FILENAME.WPS**.

Notes

The Save As option is useful when you have made a modification to an existing file and want to save both the old and new version.

When you save a file for the first time, the Save As dialog box appears automatically so that you can name the new file.

See also *Save*.

Search

Word Processor, Database, Spreadsheet

Purpose

Searches a text file, spreadsheet, or database and finds the first occurrence of the specified text or number.

To search for a word or string in a word processor file

1. Press **Ctrl-Home** to move the cursor to the beginning of the file.

2. Press **Alt** to access the menu bar.

3. From the menu bar, choose Select.

4. From the Select menu, select Search.

   The Search dialog box appears.

5. In the Search For box, type the characters for which you want to search. Also indicate whether you want the whole word matched and if you want to match the upper- and lowercase letter combination.

6. Select OK or press **Enter**.

   Works finds the first occurrence of the specified word.

7. If you want to continue the search, press **F7**.

   Works finds the next occurrence of the word.

8. Continue the search through the entire document, if you want.

   When the search reaches the end of the document, Works informs you that it can no longer find a match for the specified word.

9. When the search is complete, select OK or press **Enter** to cancel the search.

To search for a formula in a spreadsheet

1. With the spreadsheet that you want to search as the active file, press **Alt** to access the menu bar.

2. From the menu bar, select Options.

3. From the Options menu, select Show Formulas.

4. Press **Alt** again to access the menu bar.

5. From the menu bar, choose Select.

6. From the Select menu, select Search.

   The Search dialog box opens.

7. Enter the formula for which you want to search. You can type the text in upper- or lowercase letters.

8. Specify if you want to search by rows or columns. If you select columns, the search begins in column A and moves across the spreadsheet. If you select rows, the search begins in row 1 and moves down the spreadsheet.

9. Select OK or press **Enter**.

10. The cursor moves to the first occurrence of the formula.

11. Press **F7** to continue searching through the spreadsheet.

To search a database

1. Press **Alt** to access the menu bar.

2. From the menu bar, choose Select.

3. From the Select menu, choose Search.

4. When the Search For dialog box appears, enter the data for which you are searching.

5. Select either Next Record or All Records from the dialog box.

   The Next Record option enables you to find only the next occurrence of the data that you entered; no records are hidden when you select the Next Record option.

If you select All Records, Works displays the records that match the data for which you are searching. The records that do not match are hidden from view.

Notes

When searching in the word processor, you can search for specific words and character strings. When you activate the search function, Works begins searching at the location of the cursor and moves to the end of the document. You can search an entire document by moving the cursor to the beginning of the document and activating the search function. To search a specific area of text, highlight the text and activate the search function. Works will search from the beginning to the end of the highlighted text.

When searching in the database List view, you can search the entire database, selected fields, or certain records. When searching the database Form view, you can search the entire database only.

In the database, you also can search hidden records and display all the records that contain the characters for which you are searching.

You can use wild cards in searches. An asterisk (*) will find a series of characters. If you type S*, for example, Works finds all words that begin with S.

Send File

Communications

Purpose

Transmits an entire file to another computer.

To send a file

1. While connected, send the message that the other computer requires to begin receiving files.

2. Press **Alt** to access the menu bar.

3. From the menu bar, select Transfer.

4. From the Transfer menu, select Send File.

   A dialog box appears.

5. Select or type the name of the file that you are sending.

6. In the Format box, select Binary or Text file. In most transfers, you will use the Binary option. It will preserve the file as you constructed it (the formatting will remain intact, for example).

    If the file is a text file, designate the appropriate end-of-line sequence. Most of the time, you will want to use a CR (Carriage Return) and LF (Line Feed) sequence.

7. Select OK or press **Enter**.

    The file begins transferring. The status line will alternate between SEND and WAITING. Do not be surprised if transferring the file takes awhile.

8. When Works finishes sending the file, select OK to resume your work session.

Notes

When you use this procedure, the file does not appear on-screen.

To send a file, you must be connected to another computer or a service. If you are connected to another computer (a friend's computer in another office, for example), your configurations must match as to the baud rate, parity, and so on. If the configurations do match, you will use the XMODEM setting. Let the other computer know that you are ready to send the file. With a service such as CompuServe, a menu offering is available for it to be aware of your intention.

At any point in the transfer, you can stop the process by pressing **Esc**. Works responds with a dialog box asking you if you want to quit.

Send Text

Communications

Purpose

Sends data to another computer.

To send a file to another computer

1. While connected, press **Alt** to access the menu bar.

2. From the menu bar, select Transfer.

3. From the Transfer menu, select Send Text.

   The File dialog box appears, which lists word processor files. To delay text transfer, enter 1 in the Delay field. This entry shows each line of text by one-tenth of a second.

4. Type the name of the file that you want to send. If the receiving computer is slower than Works, you can slow the transfer by entering a value in the Delay box.

5. Select OK or press **Enter**.

Note

The Send Text command sends the file as ASCII text only. Therefore, you must format any file as ASCII before you can send it.

Set Print Area

Spreadsheet

Purpose

Designates the specific spreadsheet rows and columns to print.

To set a print area

1. From within the spreadsheet, select the rows and columns that you want to print by pressing and holding the **Shift** key and then using the arrow keys to highlight the area that you want to print.

2. Press **Alt** to access the menu bar.

3. From the menu bar, select Print.

4. From the Print menu, select Print Area.

Notes

If you do not set a print area, the entire file prints.

See also *Print*.

Show All Characters

Word Processor

Purpose

Displays all characters on-screen, including formatting characters such as tab symbols and carriage returns.

To toggle the characters on or off

1. Press **Alt** to access the menu bar.

2. From the menu bar, select **O**ptions.

3. From the Options menu, select Show All Characters.

   The menu disappears. If Show All Characters is toggled on, all characters appear on-screen, including formatting characters. If Show All Characters is toggled off, only characters that you have entered appear on-screen.

Notes

The diamond appears next to Show All Characters on the menu to indicate that this option is On.

With the Show All Characters command set to On, Tabs are indicated in the text with →, and paragraphs are indicated with ¶.

Show All Records

Database

Purpose

Redisplays hidden records.

To redisplay hidden records

1. Press **Alt** to access the menu bar.

2. From the menu bar, choose **S**elect.

3. From the Select menu, choose Show All Records.

Notes

Use this command before viewing or printing a report that requires the use of all database records.

When you use the Show All Records option, you do not delete the active query. It is still available to you. Press **Alt** to access the menu bar, choose **S**elect, and select Apply **Q**uery.

Show Footnotes

Word Processor

Purpose

Displays footnotes on-screen so that you can edit them.

To display footnotes on-screen

1. Press **Alt** to access the menu bar.

2. From the menu bar, select **O**ptions.

3. From the Options menu, select Show Footnotes.

   When turned on, the formatted footnotes appear on-screen. When turned off, the formatted footnotes are hidden.

Notes

The Show Footnotes option works like a toggle. Select the option again to turn it off.

If you have not created any footnotes, you cannot select this option.

To access a footnote, press **F6**. To return to the document, press **F6** again.

Show Formulas

Spreadsheet

Purpose

Displays the formulas created for a spreadsheet, not the calculated values, on-screen.

To display the spreadsheet formulas

1. Press **Alt** to access the menu bar.

2. From the menu bar, select **O**ptions.

3. From the Options menu, select Show **F**ormulas.

   When the diamond appears next to the Show Formulas option, formulas—not calculated values—appear in cells.

Notes

The Show Formulas option works like a toggle. To turn off the option, select it again.

Use the Show Formulas option to find errors in a spreadsheet or to understand better how a spreadsheet works.

Show Ruler

Word Processor

Purpose

Displays the on-screen ruler.

To display the on-screen ruler

1. Press **Alt** to access the menu bar.

2. From the menu bar, select **O**ptions.

3. From the Options menu, select Show **R**uler.

Notes

The Show Ruler option works like a toggle. If you no longer want the ruler to display, select the option again.

If you toggle the ruler on, the menu disappears and the ruler appears on-screen. If you toggle the ruler off, the ruler disappears from the screen.

The numbers in the ruler line indicate the position of the tab stops and the [ ] indicates the position of the margins.

A diamond appears next to Show Ruler on the menu to indicate that this option is on. When on, the ruler appears on-screen.

Sign-On

Communications

Purpose

Plays back a recorded sign-on sequence of keystrokes.

To play back a sign-on sequence

1. Connect to the other computer.

2. At the point at which you previously recorded the sign-on, press **Alt** to access the menu bar.

3. From the menu bar, select **C**onnect.

4. From the list of recorded sign-ons, select the one that you want and press **Enter**.

Notes

Use this command at the exact same spot as when it was recorded. This means that you must have recorded a sign-on previously.

See also *Record Sign-On.*

Size

All

Purpose

Enlarges or reduces the display size of the current window.

To change the size of the current window

1. Press **Alt** to access the menu bar.

2. From the menu bar, select Window.

3. From the Window menu, select Size.

4. Use the arrow keys to move the bottom right corner of the window in the direction that you want the sides to move.

   If you are using a mouse, drag the lower right corner of the window until it is the size that you want.

5. Press **Enter**.

Notes

When you use the Size command, the bottom and right sides of the window move in response to your pressing the arrow keys.

The smallest horizontal size the window can be is three lines; the smallest vertical size is 20 characters.

Sort Records

Spreadsheet, Database

Purpose

Reorders the records in the database or the rows in a spreadsheet.

To change the database sort order, the report sort order, or the rows in the spreadsheet

1. Press **Alt** to access the menu bar.

2. From the menu bar, choose Select.

3. In the database, select Sort Records.

4. In the First Field box, type the name of the field to sort if it is different from the proposed field name.

5. Select ascending or descending order.

6. To sort an additional field, repeat steps 2 and 3.

7. Choose OK or press **Enter**.

To sort rows or columns in a spreadsheet

1. Highlight the area to be sorted by pressing and holding the Shift key and then pressing the arrow keys.

2. Press **Alt** to access the menu bar.

3. From the menu bar, choose Select.

4. From the Select menu, choose Sort Rows.

5. Determine the sort order by making entries in the Sort Order dialog box.

6. Select OK or press **Enter**.

Notes

You can reorder the records or rows in ascending or descending order. Works can sort records using up to three fields at a time or, in a spreadsheet, three columns at a time. The sort fields that you set in Report view do not change the sort fields that you set in List or Form view. Each report can have its own sort settings.

See also *Form* and *List*.

Split

Word Processor, Database, Spreadsheet

Purpose

Enables you to see different parts of the same file simultaneously.

To split the current window

1. Press **Alt** to access the menu bar.

2. From the menu bar, select Window.

3. From the Window menu, select Split.

4. Use the arrow keys to move the split to where you want it.

5. Press **Enter**.

If you use a mouse, drag the split bar in the scroll bar to where you want the split.

6. Press **F6** or **Shift-F6** to move the cursor from one pane to another.

If you use a mouse, click the pane that you want.

Notes

In the spreadsheet and database, you may split the current window horizontally and vertically. In the word processor, you may split the current window horizontally.

Conceptually, splitting the window creates different window panes that enable you to see distinct parts of a file simultaneously.

= Style

Spreadsheet, Database

Purpose

Sets a format for the alignment of text and numbers, applies styles, and locks the contents of selected cells or fields.

To modify the style in a spreadsheet

1. Select the area that you want to modify by pressing and holding the **Shift** key and then pressing the arrow keys.

2. Press **Alt** to access the menu bar.

3. From the menu bar, select Format.

4. From the Format menu, select Style.

The Styles dialog box appears. The box contains several different style options.

5. Move the cursor to the type of Alignment that you want for the selected text. You can choose one of the following types of alignment:

- General
- Left
- Right
- Centered

Press the **space bar** to select the type of alignment that you want. A bullet appears in the parentheses before your choice.

6. Move the cursor to the Style that you want for the selected text. You can choose as many of the following styles as you want:

   - Bold
   - Underline
   - Italic

   Press the **space bar** to make your choice or choices. A dash appears in the brackets before the options that you select.

7. Move the cursor to the Locked field. If you want to protect this data from changes, press the **space bar**. A dash appears in the brackets before the option.

8. Select OK or press **Enter**.

To modify the style in a database

1. Select the area that you want to modify by pressing and holding the **Shift** key and then pressing the arrow keys.

2. Press **Alt** to access the menu bar.

3. From the menu bar, select Format.

4. From the Format menu, select Style.

   The Styles dialog box appears. The box contains several different style options.

5. Move the cursor to the Alignment that you want for the selected text. You can choose one of the following types of alignment:

   - Left
   - Right

- Centered

- Justified

Press the **space bar** to select the type of alignment that you want. A bullet appears in the parentheses before your choice.

6. Move the cursor to the Style that you want for the selected text. You can choose as many of the following styles as you want:

   - Bold

   - Underline

   - Italic

   Press the **space bar** to make your choice or choices. A dash appears in the brackets before the options that you select.

7. Move the cursor to the Locked field. If you want to protect this data from changes, press the **space bar**. An X appears in the brackets before the option.

8. Move the cursor to the Slide to Left option. If you want text to slide to the left when you print the database so that less blank space prints, press the **space bar**. An X appears in the brackets before this option.

   The Slide to Left option is available only on the Form view of a database.

9. Select OK or press **Enter**.

Note

When you are in graphics mode, the styles appear on-screen. Otherwise, they appear in the printed document only.

Switch Hidden Records

Database

Purpose

Displays hidden records and hides visible records.

To display hidden records

1. Press **Alt** to access the menu bar.

2. From the menu bar, choose Select.

3. From the Select menu, choose Switch Hidden Records.

Notes

Use this command to switch displayed records with records that are hidden by a query, a search, or by the Hide Record command.

See also *Hide Record*.

Tabs

Word Processor

Purpose

Sets, moves, or deletes tab stops. Enables you to change alignment and leader characters for tab stops and to change the distance between current tab stops.

To change a tab stop

1. Either access the menu bar and use the Select menu to select the text you want to affect, or move the cursor to the paragraph for which you want to change tabs.

2. Press **Alt** to access the menu bar.

3. From the menu bar, select Format.

4. From the Format menu, select Tabs.

5. Enter the options you want in the dialog box.

   The Tab dialog box contains the following options:

Option	Function
Position	Enables you to specify the number of the tab stop that is to be modified. Distance is measured from the left margin.

Option	Function
Alignment	Enables you to specify the type of alignment. Left positions the left edge of the text at the tab stop. Center centers the text on the tab stop. Right positions the right edge of the text at the tab stop. Decimal positions the decimal point of each entry at the tab stop.
Leader	Enables you to select the leader that you want to print in front of the tab stop.

6. Press **Enter**.

Notes

Use tab stops to align text or columns of numbers precisely, particularly when using proportional fonts. The tab stops apply only to a selected paragraph or to the paragraph in which the cursor is located.

Works applies the new tab stops to the current paragraph or to paragraphs that you have selected with the **Shift-Tab** keys.

Terminal

Communications

Purpose

Specifies the type of terminal that you are using, the terminal settings, and the size of a buffer.

To set up your Terminal options

1. Press **Alt** to access the menu bar.

2. From the menu bar, select **Options**.

3. From the Options menu, select **Terminal**.

The Terminal dialog box appears. The dialog box contains the following options:

Option	Function
Terminal	Enables you to specify either VT52 or ANSI.VT52 is the most common option.
Add Line	Enables you, when you import a text file, to add a carriage return to each line of text or to add a line feed.
Buffer	Enables you to select the size buffer that you think you may need for incoming text. The buffer is set up in RAM and therefore is dependent on your hardware. You should transfer very large files directly to disk.
Local Echo	Causes Works to display the characters you type when communicating with another computer.
Wraparound	Breaks incoming text at 80 characters per line.
Full Screen	Removes the menu bar, status line, and message line, which enlarges the terminal window display.

4. Change your settings to match those of the computer with which you are going to communicate.

5. Select OK or press **Enter**.

Note

The settings for this command can be determined by the computer to which you are planning to connect. If you are unsure of the settings for the other computer, dial into it and experiment with the settings while you are on-line.

Text

Word Processor, Communications

Purpose

Selects text for formatting, deleting, or copying.

To select text

1. Move the cursor to the place in the text where you want to begin the selection.

2. Press **Alt** to access the menu bar.

3. From the menu bar, choose Select.

4. From the Select menu, choose Text.

5. Use the arrow keys to move the cursor to the place in the text where you want the selection to end.

6. Press **Esc** to end the selection.

Notes

In the Communications module, you must be in Pause mode or disconnected from another computer to use the Text command.

You may use the **F8** shortcut key to begin selecting text.

Thesaurus

Word Processor

Purpose

Enables you to view and select synonyms that help you improve your clarity, style, and variety when writing.

To view and select a synonym

1. From within the word processor document, place the cursor anywhere on a word for which you want a synonym.

2. Press **Alt** to access the menu bar.

3. From the menu bar, select Options.

4. From the Options menu, select Thesaurus.

    The Meanings dialog box appears, which lists the meanings of the word, its part of speech, and several synonyms.

5. Highlight the synonym that you want to use to replace the word in your text and press **Enter** or **Alt-C**.

    Works enters the new word into the text and adjusts the rest of the document to fit. Press **Alt-S** to see other synonyms. If you decide you do not want to use any of the suggested works, press **Esc**.

6. Press **Alt-C** to insert the new word.

    If you want to leave the current word as it is, press **Esc**.

Note

You also can search for the synonym of a synonym that is listed in the Thesaurus. With one synonym highlighted, press **Alt-S**. Works lists any synonyms for the selected word, and you can make a choice from the list.

Time and Date

Spreadsheet, Database

Purpose

Automatically inserts the time or date into the document. Enables you to specify the format in which you want the time and date to appear.

To insert the time and date into a spreadsheet or database

1. Position the cursor in the spreadsheet cell or record in which you want the time or date to appear.

2. Press **Alt** to access the menu bar.

3. From the menu bar, select Format.

4. From the Format menu, select Time/Date.

5. From the Time/Date dialog box, select the format in

which you want the time and date to appear. You can select from the following formats:

Format	Contents
Short	Month, day, year (06/30/67)
	Month, year (06/67)
	Month, day (06/30)
Long	Month, day, year (June 30, 1967)
	Month, year (June, 1967)
	Month, day (June 30)
	Month only (June)
12-hour	Hour, minute, second (11:46:00PM)
	Hour, minute (11:46PM)
	Hour only (11PM)
24-hour	Hour, minute, second (23:46:00)
	Hour, minute (23:46)

6. Press **Enter**.

The field data cell is formatted. You now can type a date or time—depending on which you selected—in any format, and it will appear in a standard format every time. For example, suppose that you selected the Long month, day, year format. You could type **10/15/91**, and it would appear as `Oct 15, 1991`.

Notes

If you enter a time or date format into a spreadsheet cell that is too large for the cell width, Works displays # signs across the cell until you change the width.

You can insert the current date and time into a spreadsheet cell with shortcut keys. To insert the current date, press **Ctrl-+;**. You must press all three keys simultaneously. To insert the current time, press **Ctrl-+:**.

You can insert the current time and date into a database cell. To insert the current time, begin with the cursor in a field attribute location in the Form view or a cell in the List view. Press **Ctrl**-;. You must press both keys simultaneously. To insert the current date, press **Ctrl-Shift**-;.

The time or date is entered based on the computer's internal clock or based on the date and time that you entered when starting the computer at the Date and Time DOS prompts. These quick entries do not update automatically when Works performs a recalculation.

Typing Replaces Selection

Word Processor

Purpose

Toggles between Overtype mode, where highlighted text is replaced by new text that you type, and Insert mode, where original text is moved to the right and new text is inserted to the left.

To toggle the Typing Replaces Selection on or off

1. Press **Alt** to access the menu bar.
2. From the menu bar, select **O**ptions.
3. From the Options menu, select Ty ping Replaces Selection.

Note

When toggled on (Overstrike mode), new text types over already entered text. When toggled off (Insert mode), new text is inserted and the original text remains intact.

Undo

Word Processor

Purpose

Reverses the most recent action in word processing. Permits you a way to reverse editing mistakes, such as accidentally deleting a paragraph.

To reverse an action

1. Immediately after making the mistake, press **Alt** to access the menu bar.

2. From the menu bar, select **E**dit.

3. From the Edit menu, select Undo.

   Works reverses the previous editing action.

Notes

You must use the Undo command immediately after you make a mistake. If you perform any new actions between the error and the Undo command, you cannot reverse the mistake.

Undo reverses most editing and formatting actions. The command enables you to undo all commands on the Format menu; all commands on the Edit menu (except Bookmark Name and Undo); and all corrected words on the Spell Checking command.

Works Settings

Works opening screen, All

Purpose

Customizes settings in the screen display, including the language used, standard units, screen colors, number of lines on-screen, templates, modem ports, dial types, and screen mode.

To change settings

1. Press **Alt** to access the menu bar.

2. From the menu bar, select **O**ptions.

3. From the Options menu, select **W**orks Settings.

   The Works Settings dialog box appears with the following options:

Option	*Function*
Country	Enables you to select the setting that reflects your location of the work you are doing. When you change the option, the preset items that are listed change to fit the standard in the selected country. The default setting is US.
	The page size adjusts to the standard in the selected country. The default values in the Page Setup & Margins dialog box are affected.
	The standard currency symbol and display format is adjusted to the country in the spreadsheet and database.
	Wherever Works prints or displays the date and time, the order and format adjust to the selected country standard. Several other miscellaneous items adjust, also.
	If you select a country with another language, some of the characters change to the selected language.
Units	Enables you to specify the manner in which offsets are calculated for margins and so on. The default for most numbers that have units is Inches. If you enter .5 in the Tab box, for example, Works assumes that you mean 1/2 inch. Likewise, if you enter 2 cm, Works converts the measurement to .787 inches. To change the setting, select the unit that you prefer; the selected unit then becomes the default.

Option	Function
Screen Colors	Enables you to select one of three color schemes, depending on which is the easiest for you to work with. You can only use this option if you have a color system.
Lines	Specifies the number of lines that display on-screen. The standard is 25 lines per screen. You can select either 25 or 43 lines per screen.
Use Templates	Automatically loads a template that you design when you create a new file. You may design templates, which are outlines, for each of the Works tools.
Modem Port	Identifies the port to which your modem is connected, if you have a modem.
Dial Type	Specifies the type of phone system that you are using. You can use either Tone or Pulse. Generally, the setting should be Pulse.
Screen Mode	Specifies if you are working in Text or Graphics mode. Select Graphics and the mouse pointer appears as an arrow. The character styles appear on-screen (for example, the character style appears bold on-screen), and some formatting lines are visible.

Option   *Function*

Select Text and the mouse pointer
appears as a rectangle. The character
styles appear in different colors
(providing that you have a color
monitor). Some editing functions are
faster in Text mode than in Graphics
mode. You may prefer to create a
document in Text mode and then
add the finishing touches in
Graphics mode.

Press **Alt-G** for Graphics mode or
Alt-X for Text mode.

4. Press **Tab** to move the various options in the dialog
   box. Use ↑ and ↓ to move to one of the choices
   available for each option.

5. When the settings are customized, press **Tab** to move
   to the <OK> at the bottom of the dialog box. Press
   Enter.

Note

The Works Settings dialog box is specific to your video
card and your hardware.

Wrap For Screen

Word Processor

Purpose

Causes Works to display the text in the same way as it
will look when printed in regard to the number of
characters per inch. The default setting is 10 characters
per inch. However, when you use the Insert Special
command found on the Edit menu, the way text is
printed changes. The Wrap for Screen command
reformats the text on-screen to show the special
formatting.

To toggle the Wrap for Screen option on or off

1. Press **Alt** to access the menu bar.

2. From the menu bar, select **O**ptions.

3. From the Options menu, select **Wrap** For Screen.

   When this option is on, Works wraps the text at the margins on-screen only. When toggled off, the text is wrapped on-screen and then printed.

Note

The default screen display is 10 characters per inch. If you use Special Character Format, the wrap screen option displays the text as it will print.

MACROS

What is a macro?

A macro is a short computer program that automates a routine set of keystrokes. Macros simplify the steps required to run database reports, total spreadsheets, and create graphs or form letters.

To create a macro

The Works macro function acts as a recorder of the keystrokes that you enter to make something happen in Works. In fact, that is all the macro does. The macro plays back the keystrokes that you pressed in Works.

The macro is stored under a specific name, and you can replay it by pressing specific keys together. For example, you may use the **Ctrl** and **T** keys to name a macro that adds a total of numbers in a spreadsheet.

To reach the Macro dialog box, press **Alt-/** (press and hold the **Alt** key while you press the slash key). You must press these two keys together. If you have a separate numeric keypad, the slash (/) key on the keypad will not work.

The Macro Dialog Box

The Macro dialog box appears when you press Alt-/.
The box contains the following options.

Record Macro

The Works Record Macro feature is like a tape recorder;
the difference is that a tape recorder captures sound, and
the macro recorder captures input from the keyboard. If
you select the Record Macro option, the dialog box exits
the screen, and from that point on, every keyboard input
is recorded. RECORD displays on the status line in the
lower right corner of the screen, which tells you that the
Record Macro option is functioning.

The RECORD indicator remains until you reopen the
Macro dialog box and select the End Recording option.

Play Macro

This option opens a dialog box that lists all the macros
that you have created. Because you can open the Macro
dialog box at any time, you can replay any of the listed
macros. If you create a macro to save a file, for example,
you can replay it in the spreadsheet, word processor, and
database. To replay a listed macro, move the highlight to
the macro name and press Alt-P.

Skip Macro

If you created a macro and assigned its playback as a
key that is also used by Works (the F1 Help key is an
example), you can stop the macro from running at the
wrong time and still have the macro stored where you
desire.

One method is to select the Skip Macro option. When
the dialog box closes, press the keystroke that would
play back the macro normally. Works ignores the macro
playback once. If you reinvoke the macro key a second
time, it plays the macro.

The second method for shutting off the macro key is to
type an accent grave (`). The key is usually located in
the upper left corner of the keyboard. The accent grave
symbol shares the key with the tilde symbol (~). Press

the accent grave key, followed by the macro key. This procedure shuts off the macro key for one use and then returns to the macro playback function. As a general rule, do not use function keys by themselves as macro keys. Add a second key preceding the function key.

Delete Macros

The Delete Macros option erases the keystrokes recorded to a particular key. This option frees the assigned key so that it is no longer assigned to a macro. You then can use the key again for another macro.

Change Key & Title

The Change Key & Title option provides you flexibility in designating the particular key for a macro and changing the macro title, if necessary. Selecting this option opens the Macro List dialog box so that you can select the macro to be modified.

Turn Macros Off

At some point, you may want to turn off all the macros that you have recorded. The Turn Macros Off option is a toggle. Selecting the option once turns the macros off. Select the Macro dialog box again, and the option displays as Turn Macros On.

Word Processor Macros

Word processing macros are useful. If you write often, you can record addresses, favorite phrases, or entire letters in a macro. Many people use macros to record words that they frequently use or words that they often misspell. Commonly used words may include the names of companies or jargon.

To create a word processor macro

1. Open the Macro dialog box by pressing Alt-/.

2. Select the Record Macro option.

3. The Playback & Title dialog box appears.

At the Playback Key field, you can assign the key that you want to hold this recording. Do not use a key that you use for other purposes on a regular basis (such as a letter key). A good alternative to using single keys for storing macros is to use two-key combinations. Remember that Works uses the **Alt** key to activate the menu bar, so do not use **Alt** as part of the two-key combination. For this example, you may want to use the **Ctrl** key with another key.

4. Select the key combination for the macro. Select a key combination that is related to the macro's function. For example, if you are creating a macro that types your name, you might select **Ctrl-N**.

5. Press **Tab** to move the highlight to the Title field. Enter the title of the macro. For example, you might type **Name**.

6. Press **Enter** (or click OK). Works is now ready to record the keystrokes.

7. Enter the keyboard input moves that you want to record for the macro. For example, you might type your name.

   You can make any changes that you want because Works is recording every keystroke. Only the finished entry displays.

8. When you finish entering the keystrokes of the macro, press **Alt-/** again. Works displays a different menu in this dialog box because it recognizes that you have recorded keystrokes already.

   The first option, End Recording, is highlighted.

9. Press **Enter**. The dialog box closes, and you return to the word processing screen.

10. To test the macro, press the key combination that you assigned to the macro. For example, you might press **Ctrl-N**.

   Almost instantly, the macro executes.

Spreadsheet Macros

In the spreadsheet, a macro can accomplish a routine chore for you instantly. You even can use the macro to automate the spreadsheet for printing and copying.

To create a spreadsheet macro

1. Open the spreadsheet file.

2. Press Alt-/ to begin recording a macro.

3. Select the macro playback keys that you assign to this macro. Select a key combination that is related to the macro's function.

   For example, you might create a macro that inserts the current date and time. You could then assign Ctrl-D as the playback keys.

4. Type a title for the macro.

   For example, you might type **Inserting the Date and Time**.

5. The dialog box closes. Begin recording the macro.

   For example, if you are creating a macro to insert the current date and time, you might follow these steps:

   With the cell selector in cell A3, type =NOW( ) and press Enter.

   Now format the cell. Press Alt for the menu bar, select the Format menu, and select the Time/Date option. When the Time/Date dialog box opens, select the Month, Day, Year option and then press Enter or click OK.

   Press ↓ to make A4 the active cell. Then type =NOW( ).

   Format the cell for the time. Press Alt and then select Format. Select the Hour, Minute option from the Time/Date dialog box.

6. When you finish recording the macro, press Alt-/ to open the Macro dialog box and select End Recording.

7. Test the macro by entering the macro playback keys that you assigned to the macro.

   For example, you can run the preceding macro by pressing **Ctrl-D**. The menus flash by on the screen, and the time and date are inserted wherever the cell selector was located.

Database Macros

Databases are used frequently for performing repetitive tasks. For example, consider that investors holding various mutual funds need to be informed periodically of the status of their holdings. Not every investor has the same mutual funds, so a sort task is required for sending updates to only those clients holding a particular fund. If you have to sort the investor database by hand every time you intend to update investors on their accounts, you will never get the job done.

You can create a macro that begins the sort and then pauses for you to enter the name of a particular fund. Works then can use this fund as a selection criterion.

To create a database macro

1. Open the database file.

2. Press **Alt-/** to begin the macro recording.

3. Select the macro playback keys that you want to assign to this macro. Select a key combination that is related to the macro's function.

   For example, you might create a macro that begins a sort and then pauses so that you can enter the name of a mutual fund. You could then assign **Ctrl-S** as the playback keys.

4. Type a title for the macro.

   For example, you might type **Sort by fund**.

5. The dialog box closes. Begin recording the macro.

   As an example, you can perform a query based on the

renewal date. When the query screen appears, however, don't proceed with a date-based query. Press Alt-/. The Macro Options dialog box appears.

Select the Variable Input option, and the next time you run the macro, it will stop and wait for you to enter the new date of renewal. The date that you enter when you create the macro—or the dates that you enter when playing back the macro in subsequent months—do not become a permanent part of the macro. Every time that you use the macro, it will pause for data entry.

After entering the variable, such as as =5/89, do not press Enter. Press Alt-/ again and select OK.

Works continues recording your keystrokes. After you finish the query, have Works print a mailing label and a form letter containing the amount owned. This information also can be inserted with the variable input pause.

Use the same technique to insert a fixed input entry or a timed pause. At the point where you want the macro to stop, press Alt-/ and select the type of pause that you want.

6. When you finish recording the macro, press Alt-/ to open the Macro dialog box and select End Recording.

7. Test the macro by entering the macro playback keys that you assigned to the macro.

   For example, you can run the preceding macro by pressing Ctrl-S. The macro executes, pausing for data entry and sorting records based on that entry.

Nested Macros

A nested input macro is simply a second macro that runs inside a macro. Create the main macro, and when you have input that is repetitious, press Alt-/ to open the Macro dialog box, select Nested Input, and proceed with the second macro. Because the procedure creates a separate macro, you must designate another specific keystroke and macro name.

The nested macro is also a macro in its own right, and you can play it back by pressing the designated key or keys. You can play the nested macro independently without playing the main macro first.

Playing Macros

You also can play back the macro by using the Macro dialog box and selecting the Play Macro option. Selecting this option displays the list of available macros.

To play a macro, move the highlight to the macro that you want and press **Enter**. The macro executes. Notice that the first macro listed has no title. This omission demonstrates the advantage of adding a title to every macro that you create. If you title every macro, you can come back to a macro that you have not used for several months and remember what it does. Using macro titles is particularly important because you can write macros to do anything that Works can do.

Suppose that you create a macro to select all the text in a word processing file and then to delete it. If you fail to name the macro and then accidentally ask Works to play it back, you may delete a valuable file. To be safe, add a title to all your macros.

Modifying Macros

Every macro that you record is stored in a specific file that you can access with all Works tools. The file is a word processing file called MACROS.INI. Works creates and saves the file after you have created a macro. Prior to that, the file does not exist. You can modify the file until you first have created a macro and then exited Works.

To open the macro file

1. Close all open files.

2. Press **Alt** to access the menu bar.

3. From the menu bar, select **F**ile.

4. From the File menu, select **O**pen.

5. Type **MACROS.INI** and press **Enter**.

6. A screen message appears indicating that you cannot use macros while this file is open. Press **Enter** or select OK.

    The next screen offers you a choice of opening a word processor, database, or spreadsheet macro.

7. Select Word Processor and the macro file opens.

    Although the macro file looks complex, it contains only the recorded keystrokes with certain conventions. The asterisk (*) indicates the name of the macro. Looking closely, you can recognize the keystrokes for the macros that you created.

To edit a macro

You edit macros in the Works word processor. All the text-editing keystrokes covered in the word processing commands work for editing macros.

Refer to the Microsoft Works manual for an extensive listing of all the macro keystrokes and their individual translations into macro language. To edit or create a macro, simply modify these keystrokes as you would any word processor file.

A new macro must start with an asterisk and a title together on the same line. When you create a macro completely from the word processor, the new macro appears in the Macro List dialog box.

You cannot invoke the Macro dialog box while you are in the MACROS.INI file.

To edit the playback key or the title of the macro

1. Press **Alt-/**.

2. Use the highlight to select the macro that you want to edit.

3. Press **Alt-C** to change the macro.

4. Make any changes that you want to the macro.

To turn off all macros

1. Press **Alt-/**.

2. Select Turn Macros Off.

   The macros remain off until you return to the Macro dialog box and repeat the keystroke sequence. The option is a toggle and switches from on to off as you select it.

Repeating Macros

You can create a macro that performs the same task repeatedly without you having to restart the macro every time it completes a single task. After typing the keystrokes to make the macro work, press the same keys that you designated as the macro keys. If you used the combination **Ctrl-B**, for example, press **Ctrl-B** at the end of the macro.

The procedure creates a continuous loop where the macro continues performing. The macro may continue to invoke itself, even when all the actions desired have been completed.

When you want the macro to stop executing, simply press **Alt-/**. The macro stops.

Deleting Macros

To delete a macro, use the same dialog box that you used for the other macro options. Press **Alt-/** and select the Delete Macros option. The list of macros that you have created appears. Select the macro that you want to delete.

Press **Alt-L** when the macro that you want to delete is highlighted. Works deletes the macro.

Index

X

Discover the World's Best-Selling Computer Books From Que!

Spreadsheet Titles

1-2-3 Database Techniques	$24.95
1-2-3 Graphics Techniques	$24.95
1-2-3 Macro Library, 3rd Edition	$39.95
1-2-3 Release 2.2 QueCards	$19.95
1-2-3 Release 2.2 Quick Reference	$ 8.95
1-2-3 Release 2.2 QuickStart	$19.95
1-2-3 Release 2.2 Workbook and Disk	$29.95
1-2-3 Release 3.1 Quick Reference	$ 8.95
1-2-3 Release 3.1 QuickStart	$19.95
1-2-3 Release 3.1 Workbook and Disk	$29.95
Excel Quick Reference	$ 8.95
Excel QuickStart	$19.95
Quattro Pro Quick Reference	$ 8.95
Quattro Pro QuickStart	$19.95
Using 1-2-3/G	$29.95
Using 1-2-3, Special Edition	$27.95
Using 1-2-3 Release 2.2, Special Edition	$27.95
Using 1-2-3 Release 3.1	$29.95
Using Excel 3 for Windows	$29.95
Using Quattro Pro	$24.95
Using SuperCalc5, 2nd Edition	$29.95

Database Titles

dBASE III Plus Handbook, 2nd Edition	$24.95
dBASE III Plus Workbook and Disk	$29.95
dBASE IV PC Tutor	$39.95
dBASE IV Programming Techniques	$24.95
dBASE IV Quick Reference	$ 8.95
dBASE IV 1.1 QuickStart	$19.95
dBASE IV Workbook and Disk	$29.95
Using Clipper, 2nd Edition	$29.95
Using DataEase	$22.95
Using dBASE IV	$27.95
Using Oracle	$29.95
Using Paradox 3	$24.95
Using R:BASE	$29.95

To Order Your Que Books Today, Call:
1-800-428-5331

Business Applications Titles

Allways Quick Reference	$ 8.95
Introduction to Business Software	$14.95
Microsoft Works Quick Reference	$ 8.95
Q&A Quick Reference	$ 8.95
Que's Computer User's Dictionary	$ 9.95
Que's Wizard Book	$ 9.95
SmartWare Tips, Tricks, and Traps, 2nd Edition	$24.95
Using Enable/OA	$24.95
Using Microsoft Works: IBM Version	$22.95
Using PFS: First Choice	$22.95
Using Q&A	$27.95
Using Smart	$22.95
Using SmartWare II	$29.95
Using Symphony, Special Edition	$29.95
Using Time Line	$24.95

Finance/Accounting Titles

1-2-3 Personal Money Manager	$29.95
Quicken Quick Reference	$ 8.95
Using Andrew Tobias' TaxCut	$24.95
Using DacEasy, 2nd Edition	$22.95
Using Managing Your Money, 2nd Edition	$19.95
Using MoneyCounts	$19.95
Using Peachtree	$27.95
Using Quicken: IBM Version, 2nd Edition	$19.95
Using TurboTax	$24.95

CAD Titles

AutoCAD Quick Reference, 2nd Edition	$ 8.95
Using AutoCAD, 3rd Edition	$29.95
Using Generic CADD	$24.95

Desktop Publishing/Graphics Titles

Corel Draw Quick Reference	$ 8.95
Harvard Graphics Quick Reference	$ 8.95
Que's Using Ventura Publisher	$29.95
Using Animator	$24.95
Using DrawPerfect	$24.95
Using Harvard Graphics, 2nd Edition	$24.95
Using Freelance Plus	$24.95
Using PageMaker 4 for Windows	$29.95
Using PFS: First Publisher, 2nd Edition	$22.95
Using PowerPoint	$24.95
Using Publish It!	$24.95

Word Processing Titles

Microsoft Word 5 Quick Reference	$ 8.95
Using LetterPerfect	$22.95
Using Microsoft Word 5.5: IBM Version	$24.95
Using MultiMate	$22.95
Using PC Write	$22.95
Using Professional Write	$19.95
Using Word for Windows	$24.95
Using WordPerfect 5	$27.95
Using WordPerfect 5.1, Special Edition	$27.95
Using WordStar, 3rd Edition	$27.95
WordPerfect PC Tutor	$39.95
WordPerfect Power Pack	$39.95
WordPerfect 5 Workbook and Disk	$29.95
WordPerfect 5.1 QueCards	$19.95
WordPerfect 5.1 Quick Reference	$ 8.95
WordPerfect 5.1 QuickStart	$19.95
WordPerfect 5.1 Tips, Tricks, and Traps	$24.95
WordPerfect 5.1 Workbook and Disk	$29.95

Hardware/Utilities/Networking Titles

Fastback Quick Reference	$ 8.95
Hard Disk Quick Reference	$ 8.95
Introduction to Personal Computers	$19.95
Networking Personal Computers, 3rd Edition	$24.95
Norton Utilities Quick Reference	$ 8.95
PC Tools Quick Reference, 2nd Edition	$ 8.95
Que's PC Buyer's Guide	$12.95
Upgrading and Repairing PCs	$29.95
Using Norton Utilities	$24.95
Using Novell NetWare	$29.95
Using PC Tools Deluxe	$24.95
Using PROCOMM PLUS, 2nd Edition	$24.95
Using Prodigy	$19.95
Using Your Hard Disk	$29.95

To Order Your Que Books Today, Call:
1-800-428-5331

Operating Systems Titles

Batch File and Macros Quick Reference	$ 8.95
DOS Tips, Tricks, and Traps	$24.95
DOS Workbook and Disk, 2nd Edition	$29.95
MS-DOS PC Tutor	$39.95
MS-DOS Quick Reference	$ 8.95
MS-DOS QuickStart, 2nd Edition	$19.95
MS-DOS User's Guide, Special Edition	$29.95
Understanding UNIX: A Conceptual Guide, 2nd Edition	$21.95
Using DOS	$22.95
Using Microsoft Windows 3, 2nd Edition	$24.95
Using OS/2	$24.95
Using PC DOS, 3rd Edition	$24.95
Using UNIX	$29.95
Windows 3 Quick Reference	$ 8.95
Windows 3 QuickStart	$19.95

Macintosh/Apple II Titles

The Big Mac Book, 2nd Edition	$29.95
The Little Mac Book	$12.95
Que's Macintosh Multimedia Handbook	$29.95
Using AppleWorks, 3rd Edition	$24.95
Using Excel:Macintosh Version	$24.95
Using FileMaker	$24.95
Using MacDraw	$24.95
Using MacroMind Director	$29.95
Using MacWrite	$24.95
Using Microsoft Word 4: Macintosh Version	$24.95
Using Microsoft Works: Macintosh Version, 2nd Edition	$24.95
Using PageMaker: Macintosh Version	$24.95

Programming Language Titles

Assembly Language Quick Reference	$ 8.95
C Programmer's Toolkit	$39.95
C Quick Reference	$ 8.95
DOS and BIOS Functions Quick Reference	$ 8.95
DOS Programmer's Reference, 2nd Edition	$29.95
Network Programming in C	$29.95
Oracle Programmer's Guide	$29.95
QuickBASIC Advanced Techniques	$24.95
Turbo Pascal Advanced Techniques	$24.95
Turbo Pascal Quick Reference	$ 8.95
UNIX Programmer's Quick Reference	$ 8.95
UNIX Programmer's Reference	$29.95
UNIX Shell Commands Quick Reference	$ 8.95
Using Assembly Language, 2nd Edition	$29.95
Using BASIC	$24.95
Using C	$29.95
Using QuickBASIC 4	$24.95
Using Turbo Pascal 6, 2nd Edition	$29.95